AF269054

Other titles by the author:

On the Other Hand: The Little Anthology of Big Questions

Just Around the Bend: Más o Menos

Louder than a Whisper: Clearer than a Bell

Umbra, Penumbra & Me (a compilation)

The Doubt Factor

Children's Picture Books by this author:

The Frightened Little Flower Bud   *Ages 4-99*

Hat   *Ages 6-99*

"For what are we born if not to aid one another."
- Ernest Hemmingway

Stepping out of Time

Renée Paule

RPG Publishing

No jargon!

For your convenience there are blank pages

for notes at the back of this book.

For the fluidity of this book, I use the pronoun we a great deal. This is how I see us; we're One. Yes, it's not always appropriate to use the proverbial we, but for the purposes of this book its meaning is general.

Stepping Out of Time

By Renée Paule

Edited by G R Hewitt

Cover design and artwork by Renée Paule

Earth Image courtesy NASA Johnson Space Centre

All illustrations by Renée Paule

Written in British English

ISBN: 978-1-9162039-1-4

For Petra

Thank You

Godfrey

Dr. Adnan Khan

Hazel

Table of Contents

Preface

After writing my first book I thought that subsequent ones would be easier, but nothing could be further from the truth. The biggest hurdle was getting over the idea that others are better qualified to write what I write, but who can write of my experiences; who can possibly be better qualified to write about my world? Who is better placed to record the contradictions, nuances, influences and thought processes that have guided me from a dark past into a brighter Now? Who is better placed to guide me from both dark and light - from all dualistic conditioning? Only I can reflect on my life's experiences and through this sincere reflection which began in my childhood - albeit in a somewhat twisted way - was born a need to write about them, together with a deep and compelling need to know myself. All I can offer you in this book is an honest blend of the ways in which I see the world.

Introduction

*Change the way you see yourself and you'll
change the way you see everybody else.*

After writing three books that reflect on Humanity, I've come to realise that I'm neither closer to nor further away from discovering an 'ultimate' understanding of my world. The restlessness I feel is not something I can ignore or question - it can't be pushed aside and I've no wish to do so. It calls me - with some urgency - to reflect on the world I've created for myself and to be the best person I can be within it; I'm not here to 'solve' it and I'm not here to find answers. I'm here as my own authority and to find my way in life - not to be steered by others who may think they know what's 'best' for me. The only real waste in this world is the waste of our lives if we ignore the opportunity to make a difference - to learn to love ourselves, and through that love be able to love all others.

There's nothing in any of my books that we don't already know and for this reason I often ponder on why I'm writing them at all. It all comes down to this; I must unlearn everything I 'know' with the same rigidity that I learnt it - I must hammer at and chip away all obstacles that keep me from seeing what lies beneath my outer shell - I must break into my own safe! I can't show or tell you how to 'straighten out' your life, or how to see the magic in it. I can only show you how I'm straightening out my own life and how with careful attention to my thoughts and inner voice the noise and chaos in my mind has abated; however, it's not yet fully quiet. My journey of self-reflection has been one of observation and erasure; as you are aware, erasing ink or graphite from paper is not so easy - persistent blemishes and impressions remain.

Hello World

*We've wild imaginations, to which
there appears to be no limit.*

I don't remember when I became aware that I was aware - that 'hello world' moment when I realised I was 'here' with no introduction or explanation. To my knowledge, no-one shook my hand or welcomed me into the world. I had to observe, listen, learn a language, evolve and form images of my world before I was able to interact with it, in whatever way seemed appropriate. I imagine it might have felt like being pushed onto a stage where millions of different plays are in full swing and, from *my* point of observation, trying to play *my* part with no script or character description - learning to play a role by imitation and improvisation, so that I'd fit in. Amongst all this confusion, I was unknowingly building a character that became the *me* others would see - my persona. I allowed my mind to be filled with the beliefs, distractions, fears and influences of others and I made them 'mine'. I was to create a role for myself from the information, 'props' and people that surrounded me and regardless of my choices, the play would go on. I could observe or participate in this 'show' - fully or partially - or I could sit quietly and observe it, but I couldn't leave the 'theatre'. Thinking about this reminds me of when my father 'taught' me to swim at around four-years-old; he threw me into the deep end of a pool and told me to swim back to the side and climb out again; the ladder was very far away, as it is when we're afraid, alone and unwelcome.

I was born into chaos and not much later went into a shell, to protect myself from a strange and confusing situation, from which I could find no way out. As a young child, I can't remember at what age but I'd guess it was pre-school, I found my environment to be extremely hostile. It was an environment in which I'd no rights, choices, or a voice anyone would listen to. It was a place where I needed to 'come of age' before I'd have some sort of control over my life - control within the confines of choices that had already been made for me, by society - a very sick society that above all else, taught me how to be afraid of it and to hate myself. From my perspective at the time, the world was ugly, corrupt, violent, unjust and cruel; I'd no idea how I'd arrived or what I was doing here. I felt about as much use as a teardrop shed on a battlefield, and a tremendous sense of not belonging; there was no-one to discuss my thoughts with. I cared not for this 'home', had no wish to remain in it and because I couldn't see a way out, felt powerless to change anything. There was however, a voice that I heard all the time; a voice that told me that there was more to me than this. At the time I didn't understand the significance of this voice and like the majority of us, ignored it. Whatever this voice was - this nagging, this underlying something that I didn't understand at the time - conflicted with my circumstances and all that I was being taught about myself.

~~~
~~~

I've meditated long and hard about what it may be like for a child to enter our world and as it happens, I've had the opportunity to 'video conference' with a friend's new born baby. The baby needs a little help to face the screen, by means of a supporting hand on the back of her neck and another to gently prop her tiny body up. The first time we met, she was cross-eyed, frowning and flapping her arms and legs around frantically as though she'd suddenly found herself trapped - somewhere strange - and was trying to get out again. Yes, the movements are reflexive, but from an observer point of view this isn't clear without prior conditioning. At times the frown subsided and she'd have that cute little baby face that the vast majority of us succumb to.

However, occasionally her lips curled downwards at the sides and very shortly afterwards, she'd sob her little heart out as though her world had come to an end, rather than just begun. We turn our lips down and lower our eyebrows when we're unhappy whether we're sobbing our hearts out or not, even after growing up, so it was a part of us when we were born and, it still is. Babies don't speak a language we understand, but in my opinion, they know they've arrived somewhere new and according to the screams of some of them, they may well be more than a little confused by their new surroundings, or frustrated by their inability to communicate in any way other than to cry. They may also be frightened or in shock and want 'out' again. Of course there are those of us that don't scream out the moment we're born, but sooner or later - in one way or another - we do.

That an inexplicable BIOS (basic input/output system) exists within each of us is beyond doubt; if we didn't have one then our hearts couldn't beat, our tears couldn't flow, our lips couldn't curl and the jerky reflexive movements of our arms and legs couldn't occur; we couldn't be switched 'on', or 'off' for that matter; our hearts, tears, lips and limbs couldn't exist without the code that somehow forms and operates them. Before our births, meticulously coded instructions are carried out for every stage of our development - we couldn't live without them. To call this a system - a *basic* one at that - has got to be the biggest understatement ever made, but this is the limit that language permits us to describe the marvellous process of conception and subsequent 'life'. After our births, begins the relatively lengthy process of development, as we gradually learn how to use and control our bodies, while they continue the development process begun in the womb; the system is fully automated. There's no-one who can tell us how - or why

- we came into being, no matter how deep or extensive their learning; we can only marvel at the wonder of it all if we're prepared to spend some time reflecting on - as opposed to studying - the phenomenon itself.

What should be a sacred reverential moment has been relegated to a mechanical incident no more - or less - important or impressionable than a new car rolling off a production line. Our births are planned for by our mothers and fathers, authors, commercial outlets, doctors and midwifes and a seemingly limitless number of approved baby-by-the-book 'how to' instruction manuals. The beauty and wonder of what's happening inside a mother's body - outside our control - is often reduced to something fashionable as we now show off our 'bump' in clothing designed specifically for that purpose. When do we speak about or acknowledge the genetic wonder of it all, let alone the philosophical and spiritual aspects of our existence? When do we put aside a little of our precious time to ponder these things?

It's my considered opinion that no-one can tell us what a baby can or can't see. No-one can tell us what a baby thinks or what his mind chatters on about, in whatever language he may or may not comprehend. Thoughts are the past so a baby *must* experience *before* he can think and whether his experiences begin inside the womb or after birth is a question - like all my questions - that I shall leave open. Babies arrive and as far as we can tell, we assess what they need through their cries, emotions, temperature, breathing etc. When I was caring for my own children, knowing what they wanted at any particular moment involved a lot of guesswork and a process of elimination; not hungry, not wet etc. - often I reached the end of my 'check list' and the problem still hadn't been solved. No doubt there were things I never tried, as they were beyond my knowledge but - for the purpose of this chapter - I'm only focusing on what I see through my own eyes and through meditation, reflecting on what a baby may see or feel from her own perspective. Why is this interesting to me? Because I apparently arrived 'here' in the same way - just as we all did. Finding my truth has been a process of unlearning and it follows that in order to do so, I must end up at the beginning of my learning again, as far as is possible. I can't go back to my birth, but I don't need to; everything falls into place when we're good and ready.

Again, no-one can tell us where we came from or where we're going, whether this life is a dream, an illusion, a game, a show, or 'the real McCoy', so to speak. For me however, whatever direction my questions lead me in, I'm 'Here' at my point of observation and I can never leave. I'm at the centre of my own world from which all aspects of my life spring. As we become more proficient at observation a curious thing happens - there's a distinct feeling that we ourselves are being keenly observed and by 'we' I mean our 'egos'. I shall extend this statement to say that I feel as though I'm keenly observing *myself*.

Know Thyself

The term 'Know thyself' (γν□θι σεαυτ□ν in Greek or *nosce te ipsum* in Latin) is one of the best known phrases in the world and often pops up in books, films and social media in one form or another, but what *does* the aphorism mean? To many people, it's nothing more than an ancient mystical cliché and in general given as much thought as any other 'fortune cookie' wisdom. Little wonder most people aren't too curious about the concept of 'know thyself', regarding it as a topic to be explored by the 'select few' believed to be in the know about humanity's 'hidden' secrets; we're content to await their spectacular revelations appearing in the Sunday papers and what have you - meanwhile, life goes on as we know it. 'Know thyself' sounds more like 'know thy place' or 'know thy limitations' and don't try to reach beyond them - this is the message a lot of people receive, albeit subconsciously. To complicate matters, many of us believe we *already* know ourselves, others lack the time or inclination to think about it, rejecting it out of hand; however, to those who earnestly need to make some sort of sense out of our world, there's no option but to explore further.

The three words *know thy self* can be taken apart and all sorts of sense made out of them and many people do this, but the inescapable message is 'go within', 'look inside you' - an action we'd prefer to avoid. One thing worth recognising is how lazy we are, especially when it comes to matters of a spiritual nature - on the whole, it just doesn't interest us enough to stop what we're doing. I'd suggest this is partly out of fear - fear of failure, fear of success, fear of ridicule, inadequacy or of losing what we may have to give up. Perhaps our greatest fear is of the isolation that could result from such a quest. Friends and family often become quickly uninterested in - or annoyed at - anything we have to say regarding philosophical or spiritual matters; at best, they'll tolerate a few comments before rolling their eyes, dismissing us as cranks and changing the subject. At first this can be frustrating, but gradually we become unaffected by peer pressure to conform - it's part of our journey. Whichever way you look at the adage, 'know thyself' is a do-it-yourself *quest* and *that's* where our reticence kicks in; it sounds like a lot of hard work and we really can't be bothered, as we've more 'important' things to do.

When we think about what it means to 'know thyself' one of the first things to consider is that it's not necessary to know the 'ins and outs' of angels, demons, elves, fairies or other spirits; we don't have to uncover age-old mysteries of astrology, archaeology, science, philosophy or any other subject in order to know ourselves and we don't need to read Greek, Latin *or* hieroglyphics for that matter - we've enough trouble understanding our own language. There's no big secret; nothing essential is hidden from us and no special knowledge is needed to go within. We don't actually have to 'get into' anything at all and therein lies the problem; it's just too simple - so simple that it goes against our conditioning. The conditioning is that we need qualifications, ceremonies, costumes, rites, incense burning, to sit in strange positions, or at the feet of someone 'wiser' than we are, in order to receive 'privileged' knowledge. We may well search for someone else to shine a light on the subject for us, as we feel unqualified without some form of certificate or rite of passage, but by doing that all we'll find is the mass of contradiction and confusion that exists in our society, further muddling our minds. We can delve as deeply into the haystack as we choose to, but we'll not find 'the' truth; we'll be unable to differentiate between what is or isn't true as our minds *are* deeply conditioned - a fact that's difficult to accept.

The entangling web of knowledge is more complicated and confusing than the questions we ask and can't be trusted; at best we may favour one person's answer and decide to walk along their path with them, but that doesn't make anything they say true; it just means that, for a whole host of reasons, it suits our personal agenda to go along with what they're saying right now - it's an 'off the peg' solution. We don't need to lose ourselves in other people's adventures. We can have our own adventures and in fact, we *are* unknowingly having our own, though for most of us it doesn't seem that way, because our heads are stuck deep inside the stories and fantasies of others - we experience their adventures by proxy, like when we cheer for a football team, celebrate a celebrity's wedding, cry at someone else's bad news or get a kick out of a success story in the media. Sometimes we change dramatically after putting ourselves in what we see as 'positive' situations; like spiritual meetings, listening to a 'life coach' (I do dislike that term) or receiving good advice - like a drug; these situations often leave us feeling 'on a high'. However, when we return to our homes continuing to live the way we were living before, we return to behaving the same way too; in the same way we lose enthusiasm for a diet once the novelty has worn off; we start the diet, lose a few pounds and then diligently put them on again. When faced with a sudden personal crisis that unbalances us we reach out for any helping hand, but once our balance is regained we let go of that hand and revert to our old selves; a 'crisis repentance' causes us to become more agreeable to people who are offering help at the time.

When we look to others for guidance on our 'quest', problems can arise because one 'expert' believes a certain thing, and another has a different opinion; for example, 'there's a heaven and a hell' or 'there are no such places'. Both have their reasons for believing what they choose to believe, but neither can provide 'evidence' to substantiate their claim - leading to heated debates that are never resolved; this situation has been going on for a long time. Of course, there are more than two opinions, but I use those as simple examples to put my point across. We prefer to look *outside* of ourselves for fear of what we'll discover within, or to be more accurate, *re*-discover. The mass of contradiction and confusion that we find on the outside has created a mass of contradiction and confusion on the inside - *this* is why our minds are so difficult to silence.

We *all* possess the ability to question our existence regardless of whether we're rich, poor, young or infirm. We don't need to be 'educated' or to consult a psychiatrist, guru or any other 'expert' for guidance or advice; each and every one of us is self-sufficient when it comes to controlling our 'inner' selves - we don't even have to *know* anyone else - there exists no valid 'get-out clause'. All we have to do is 'think'; it's really that simple, but we can't see it because we've made our lives too complicated. Regardless, there remain many things that can be questioned and considered, things that can't be denied; for example, the world is in decline - we all know this. I recently picked up a DVD from a supermarket shelf and looked at the rating; it was Rated 'R' for 'strong violence, disturbing images, and sexuality' and it contained 'strong bloody violence' with a 'fit for viewing' age of '15 or more'; these are our children for goodness sake - we don't allow them alcohol or tobacco at that age for fear of damaging their health, but we're quite happy to damage their minds. *What* are we doing to our children? For that matter, what are we doing to *ourselves*? Scarily, we're living in a society where we need ratings to tell us what we can and can't do; the older we get the more qualified we are to be exposed to ever increasing 'officially' rated (thereby *officially* sanctioned) sex and 'bloody violence'. We all know how the label 'contains adult content' attracts our children and we don't do much to protect them from the temptation. If it's not suitable for our children then in what way, and by whose standards, is it suitable for *us*? I feel deeply saddened by this frightening lack of intelligent self-regulation and personal responsibility. We can't know ourselves if we continue to take a *laissez-faire* attitude to what's happening all around us, or how it effects humanity as a whole. By considering examples such as the above, we begin to see ourselves in a different light, which raises our level of consciousness.

~~~

So how can we begin to *really* know ourselves? Only by taking a long, hard and honest look in the mirror. If we want to see ourselves as we really are, then it's necessary to remove all outside factors that define us. Everything we feel, see, think, shy away from or judge when we look in a mirror is a part of how we see ourselves, including the moments of horror, disgust, emotion and vanity. A good exercise is to stand in front of that mirror and listen to the muddled up thoughts that we broadcast to ourselves when looking at our own reflection; for example, too big, small, fat, thin, short or any number of other inadequacies and self-rejecting - or self-praising - observations; when we look in the mirror, we see a mixed-up historical conglomeration of ourselves. We define ourselves by what we *choose* to focus on and what we choose to make of our lives, and it's from these choices that our lives expand. Ironically, the choices we make are not always the choices we *want* to make - too often they're guided by fear, the past or expected approval, flattery or condemnation of others. We're each a masterpiece in our own right - completely self-contained - and we've the tools to create a beautiful experience or a horror story; our bodies are merely
~~~

vessels through which we can view and interact with the life we create. Think about something that attracted you this week - something you couldn't resist like an object in a shop window or a book, a new job, a party invitation, a bottle of drink, a film, a person or even a cake. Something that pulled your attention towards it and then think about how it was possible for you to be drawn to that same thing - how it made you feel and what you were expecting - or got - from the experience; the pleasures of these experiences are short-lived, which is just one of the reasons we seek to re-experience them. Many lines have been cast with baited hooks and only we - personally - choose whether or not to take the bait; if we do, we're then hooked up for whatever experience we've chosen, and the memory of that experience becomes embedded in our minds; it becomes a part of us - a part of our story. We can choose not to take the bait that someone else has put out for us - this choice is an important one if we truly wish to know ourselves. I wish to point out that I'm *not* saying either option is right, wrong, moral or immoral - only that what we do *is* a choice.

It's not just material things and pastimes that we're attracted to (or seek out), but also emotions and ways to vent our frustrations with the world - ways in which we express or validate ourselves. Knowing ourselves involves *constant* self-observation and honesty, particularly about the things we *don't* want to know about ourselves. To see this, we need to study our own behaviour and listen to the background voices inside our heads that control our actions and reactions, particularly when we're up to mischief; for example, we may find ourselves looking to use or start an argument with a friend - often over something trivial - for a variety of reasons including a lack of honesty, manipulation, fear or even to fulfil an addiction - skilfully manoeuvring the argument to our own ends. Have you ever noticed how the voice of our conscience never bothers us *unless* we're doing the unwise? If we question why we ignore our conscience it becomes clear that our lives are 'ego driven'. 'Me' is with me all the time and when the validity of it is challenged that really gets our backs up. The ego is 'never' wrong and it's highly volatile; it's always ready to put up a wall, pounce, twist, be the loudest voice in the room or lie in defence of itself, no matter what, and if necessary, keep us up all night - tossing and turning - depriving us from the sleep we need and it'll keep doing that until we recognise it for what it really is - a fraud. It's at that moment an awful truth dawns on us - *we are* the fraud. Then we've a choice; we can ignore this 'revelation' by remaining as we are or embrace it.

~~~

The journey to 'know thyself' is a tough one - many of us can feel more than a little intimidated by this well-known phrase, but I'd like to put it into perspective. The journey is no tougher than the one we're currently undertaking; the hardest parts of it being learning to 'think straight' - without interference from our thoughts - and letting go of the character traits we so possessively hold onto; for instance, pride, suspicion, self-righteousness, fear and an unwillingness to change. On an encouraging note, our journey does become *easier*
~~~

once we get started - it brings its own rewards. Speaking from my own experience, I find I sleep better at night without all the rumblings of my mind and consequently, I awake feeling refreshed - I've become unperturbed by things that once irked and distracted me - the things I know I *can't* change and therefore, no longer expend energy trying to. I'm less inclined to be judgemental of others as I develop a greater understanding of myself. The more we understand ourselves, the more we understand others - the more we understand others, the more we realise that our world and place in it is incomprehensible at our current level of consciousness - a level that we can raise *now*, while we're still alive. On this journey, life becomes a mystery again as we notice and think about wonders we forgot about a long time ago - experiencing life rather than analysing and navigating our way through it, according to the instructions of others. If we want to find something sacred in our world we need to experience the wonder of it, rather than conceptualising it.

Think for a moment about your hands. Take a good look at them, flex your fingers, make a fist, point a finger and focus on what you're able to do with these incredible instruments. Our hands are made up of - amongst other things - muscles, tendons, nerves, veins, nails, bones, and skin - everything we do with them is by our will alone; they do exactly what we want them to do - what we *will* them to do. Who is it who instructs our feet to walk one in front of the other in concert with our balance system and eyes, so that we don't trip, fall over or walk into things? Everything we do and think is by our own free will, but we've been doing them for so long that we no longer recognise that it's *ourselves* who are in control of our bodies and the mind we allow to run riot.

As adults, we bury the child within us and should we allow it to surface again, as we invariably do, we feel self-conscious and vulnerable - especially if anyone is or may be watching. Too often we refuse to allow that vulnerability to surface again. It's terrifying to strip away our comprehensive defences, revealing the 'truth' to ourselves - that we're frauds - let alone to anyone else; yes, knowing ourselves is a time to 'face the music'. If we allow ourselves to face it, then all we really stand to lose is the torment and suffering we insist on experiencing and *willingly* re-experiencing. We hide because we're afraid and often rationalise this fear as necessary for our personal security, resisting change so as not to be seen as we really are. Our lifetimes have been spent perfecting our disguises in order to protect ourselves from rejection - a rejection we can't bear to face again. The journey to knowing ourselves is like giving ourselves a mental make-over; however, because of our fears of rejection, humiliation and isolation - the undesirable possible consequences of walking away from the 'crowd' - we're reticent to take this step. When we jump into the 'mind drama' our fears soon multiply into a dread story that we serialise beyond reasonable recognition - our rationalisation is complete. Life is a journey between two points - birth and death; what we do between them is important. Do you remember what the majority of us were taught in school about how to cross a road? Look right, look left, look right again listening all the time and if there's nothing coming you can cross, but continue to look and listen while you're doing it. This advice applies to our life's journey too, but, unwisely, we're not looking where we're going - we're not listening either.

Assimilation and Dissemination

We're here to experience this life; to pass through it - not to carve ourselves in stone.

Preparation for a child's arrival involves having all the correct equipment prepared, which if we take a moment to think about, isn't very different to having a new doll with all the latest accessories needed to comply with the current requirements demanded by our consumerist society. The 'advancement' and desires of humanity have caused us to need more and more things for every baby that's 'born', despite the baby's needs remaining the same as they always have been - food, covering and above all, love. However, these 'designer' babies are the only way for society to continue 'advancing' in the way it wants to - they'll one day replace our generation, just as we've replaced previous ones. If we were to teach our children 'new' things, or rather not teach them the old, then we wouldn't be able to hold onto society the way it is now. Despite protestations that we don't like things the way they are, we don't *want* to change them - particularly if it involves the personal sacrifice of any of our firmly-held 'secure' beliefs. A sick society can't teach the next generation to be healthy. Another stumbling block to change is that we don't know *how* to and we're more than a little afraid to find out. We're afraid of criticism, of losing a 'reputation' or the 'approval' of society, so we conform and seek the only apparent reasons for living the way we do - seeking continuity and success! Consequently, we continue to be unhappy while we hope to find this 'success' in our world - every one of us knows it doesn't actually exist.

Start to look at the world objectively and it becomes impossible not to see that the vast majority of us (if not all) suffer in one way or another. Each of us has absorbed and owns an 'eventful' past, full of imprinted memories that tell us who we think we are and who we've been told we are - but they're *not* who we are any more than the words of a story are the book they're written in. The events are and can only be what we've *experienced*, by whatever means - yet, they're how we define ourselves. I'm known as Renée Paule and she is the *sum* of my experiences - nothing more. Our story began - in part - with the nouns, verbs and adjectives that we later came to know as our 'identity'. We begin to see how our egos were formed when we weave in our emotions, pains, judgements, desires, disappointments and expectations to the story. When we see the pattern - how our characters have evolved - distances, barriers, distinctions and illusions fall away - sometimes slowly, sometimes uncomfortably fast, leaving us somewhat disorientated and possibly disturbed by our new surroundings.

Our grasping hands, reaching out for the familiar, pass through the things we once 'knew' were solid. These include our beliefs, opinions, choices and aspirations - things we thought were *ours* turn out to be nothing of the sort. As the barriers between reality and illusion are removed, we're left naked and exposed - stripped from the fine clothes we've unknowingly been dressed in for so long, with nowhere to run for cover. In this raw state we tend to grab at our old clothes, hastily putting them back on again, because they're preferable to this new and unfamiliar vulnerability - 'blind panic' causes us to cling to them for dear life. If only we'd pause, relax and take a moment to look around us, we'd soon find that our new situation isn't as frightening as it first seems. On the contrary, it liberates us from fear - there's nothing lurking 'under the bed'. We weren't born afraid - we were taught it. By a process of reverse engineering our beliefs can be deconstructed, and once we accept this raw state all fear leaves us - every little bit of it.

My perspective on what it means to be a human being has changed considerably with the examination and reflection of myself. For years, being a 'human being' limited me to being something apparently solid - something tangible. It's a term that implies the objectification of 'myself' and I'm not an object - neither are you. Our characters, thoughts etc. are anything but solid, as we tend to understand the term. The 'idea' of a human being is a wonderful thing; the idea that we're humane, compassionate, sympathetic, benevolent and special, above all others in the universe is an attractive one. The reality however, within the confines of our comprehension, is very different; though we've the potential to be all these things, we don't live up to those challenging descriptions. For benevolence to exist for example, then paradoxically, so must cruelty. Physically, the reality of being a human being is that we perform functions and routines, mimic fads and other behaviours that we're shown through our various forms of media and social interactions, and follow the influences, orders and rules of others; our conditioned behaviour is not unlike that of automatons. Psychologically, we ignore our consciences as they interfere rather too much with our desires - too often we don't *want* to hear the voice of our conscience and have been taught too well *not* to listen to it.

It isn't only our behaviour that's conditioned, but so are our thoughts and beliefs; the three are inseparable and arise from an accumulation of information perceived and digested from the moment we were 'born' until now. The cache of this information goes back many millennia and has always been passed on - it's tradition. Tradition is the passing on of any psychological or physical behaviour; it doesn't depend on truth of any kind, only the continuity of its doctrines and practices - tradition has its own agenda. It's natural for us to imitate others - how else would we learn about our world. A young child is taught everything; for example, language, right, wrong, funny, history, expectation, prejudice and many other societal driven behaviours. Here's one example; I saw a video with lots of babies giggling and laughing during different simple situations. In one scenario a baby burst into laughter when his father changed channel on the television after asking the child if he was 'Ready!' Then the mother asked the baby if he was 'watching golf' and the laughter was replaced by a look of innocent puzzlement. This is just one example of early programming and how we project what we want to believe onto our children. For me, the child was highly amused by the 'magic' trick the father was able to perform - changing the image on a screen with a little fun and anticipation thrown in. The mother, on the other hand, observed the child's excitement, took him out of the moment, translated it into something more appropriate to her own particular conditioning and in doing so, stole the innocence. Society would be all the wiser if it watched and learnt from its children, rather than manipulating them - they have a lot to teach us that we've sadly forgotten about.

~~~

A baby wouldn't survive if left unattended; without social influence/guidance or care. Apart from the obvious problems of a child being unable to find food, shelter and clothing, it would be unable to gain a perspective of the world - unable to develop a sense of identity - it would certainly die. So mimicry - with subtle changes - is essential for our survival and if we're mimicking an
~~~

unhealthy world, then that's the world we'll continue to create and live in. Our disturbed world - plus the conditioning that children come across in theirs, is the world they'll inherit. If we continue to 'enhance' our insane world then things can only get worse. Thinking about these things gives a whole new meaning to idioms like 'walking in his father's footsteps' - a whole new perspective that's far from limited to members of our family, but also to anyone we interact with. The key to change must therefore lie in the reflection and evolvement of our *own* behaviour, otherwise we'll continue to pass this contaminated 'baggage' onto our children.

I remember - during an interesting discussion - being told by a friend 'I know my own mind'. No, we don't. If we did we wouldn't put up that argument. We don't tend to recognise that our entire life has been a subjective experience - absorbing information from the minds of those we've come into contact with, either personally or by proxy. To know our own mind takes a tremendous amount of honest self-reflection and observation. It involves, but is not limited to, seeing in ourselves what we see in others and coming clean about things we know to be false, but pretend are true - particularly about ourselves. The way we interact in our environment or with other people isn't us being *us* but a conditioned response to the circumstance we find ourselves in at any particular moment, based on our previous experiences - responses that we automatically, but unknowingly access. When we taste a lemon for example, we already know the response because we've tasted it before - we know it's going to taste sour and pull the appropriate 'squeezed' up face that we've come to associate with 'sour', though the face has nothing to do with sour itself - we tend to overact the part.

Another example is what a baby learns when he makes a mess of his dinner all over the highchair. A mother may react as though it were a crisis or just calmly clean it up. Whichever reaction she has imprints on to the child so that; for example, if a second child arrives in the household and then makes the same mess the first will react as its mother did - impersonating her and projecting her learnt behaviour. We think we're in control of our minds, but nothing could be further from the truth; we're reluctant to hear this fact.

We see, and absorb incalculable amounts of information from an incalculable number of sources, as we navigate our way through the chaos and hostility of our world. In some ways, we're like sponges. We absorb and process this information squeezing out any that's excess to our particular requirements - for political, religious, educational, scientific or any other cultural conditioning we happen to find ourselves connected to. This information brings us into line with whatever criteria a particular cultural group requires us to absorb, adapting ourselves so that we're 'tuned' into their hierarchical chain, making us socially or professionally acceptable, either low in the so-called 'pecking order' as the silent majority or, higher up as an administrator of continuity and progression. Our purpose - in society - is to function as a cog; this perpetuates a cruel and ritualistic existence where an 'individual' has no actual value, beyond a 'grade' awarded to those who are happy to fall 'in line' - replacing their predecessors.

For instance, a student of a particular discipline may well wish to become a professor and will therefore continue to teach the same information his tutor taught him - rarely (publicly) questioning the reliability of the information. In some cases, this information can radically change; for example, we've been taught that people once believed the earth to be flat; however, who can honestly say that it's a globe, and if we do believe it, on what grounds do we trust that information? Based on our own evidence, who amongst us is able to verify one hundred percent that we're living on a planet at all?

In keeping with my philosophy, I maintain that answers don't need to be found in order to 'unravel' our minds from the 'Big Bang' of useless, unnecessary, diverting, corrupt and conflicting information. Our minds are so full of these things that we've become overwhelmed with too many 'truths' and 'realities' - so much so that the difference between fantasy, augmented reality, virtual reality, or 'reality' itself has become increasingly blurred. When our minds quieten, all arguments - whatever their origin - become null and void. If we see and admit to the problems, then the 'solutions' will present themselves all in good time, but *only* when we're ready to receive them. If we choose however, to remain in hiding and denial from the obvious maladies of society, then we also choose to remain as blindfolded passengers on a ship - that we *choose* to sail in - without caring in which direction we're being led by its captain, or the state of that captain's mind - we also refuse to acknowledge that there *is* a captain at all. Who is the captain? That's a good question!

Our characters have been formed to function in a low vibrational world; it's a world that shapes and conditions us according to its wishes and a world that insists not only on our compliance, but that we pass our conditioning, fears and compliance onto our offspring. We're taught that 'knowledge is power', but *what* knowledge and *whose* knowledge is not something we tend to think about or whether or not this knowledge is true - regardless, we accept it as truth. True power and knowledge is not something that we can learn from books or inherit from others - it can be found in the hearts of each and every one of us, because *that's* where it resides and where it has *always* resided. Realising and accepting this situation is the hardest part of knowing ourselves, because it's difficult to accept that the person we thought was 'uniquely' us, was moulded by the society we're living in and that in many respects, we really are just following a script. The first move to 'know thy *self*' is to question, question, and question again - everything that we've been taught without bias, without conditioning, without getting all hot and bothered and without lashing out at the system - after all, it was us who created it. We must wipe our slate clean and to begin with it's not an easy process, because we *have* to realise the futility of the way we've been living before we see anything new. Persevere, and our world changes into a far more beautiful and meaningful place to live in - this is *not* a hypothetical statement.

Memory and Thought

*There's no suvvch thing as dirty water -
despite contaminants, its essence remains
pure.*

You may be thinking about the above quote - trying to work out if it's true or not. Drawing on information stored in your memory you may come to an 'agree' or 'disagree' conclusion, or maybe you'll want to think about it some more. Every moment of our lives we're thinking about something; some of these thoughts bring pleasure and some can be so disturbing that it's hard to believe we're having them. From the moment we wake up to the moment we fall asleep, and on into the dream world, our brains are working away at something - the cogs keep turning. There are times we're so deep in thought that the world around us disappears as we go further into our minds, perhaps to wrestle with some problem, re-live an occasion or to seek escape - whatever reason, it's our private space and we retreat to it often. There are other times when we can't escape our thoughts rambling on and on, accusing us, berating us, reminding us - over and over we replay them like a stuck record; if only we could silence the incessant chatter we'd get some peace of mind. Temporary escape may come by turning on our radio or television or by going out into the noise of the street, hoping that on our return we'll find welcome silence. Whatever we think about, we do by accessing memories - our past - and when we turn to distractions we *add* to and *edit* those memories, thus causing more noise rather than alleviating it. Every thought we think belongs to us *if* we adopt it; if we think negative thoughts and see negative images then *negativity* becomes the state of our mind. We can't exist without thinking; everything we do, say, see, smell or touch involves thought and once experienced, becomes a new memory - what we look back on and forward to. Our thoughts control our decisions, so it's important to watch them closely as they arise, question where they come from, and to follow that question through.

Reflecting on 'memory' and 'thought' is something that's occupied me for many years. At first, I was confounded as I became aware of my own thoughts and began to think about the thinking process. It seemed as though there was a disconnection from myself whenever I thought on the questions; who's doing the thinking, what *is* thinking, what *is* a thought and how is it that I'm able to *think* about thinking? The deeper I delved into these questions the more confused I became - not because it was complicated but because I'd never thought about it before. I also became increasingly aware that to go further along my 'path', I had to erase every trace of 'me'. 'Me' is what I've *become* and the 'construct' for 'me' contains all the information I've ever absorbed and held onto - information stuck like 'reminder notes' (memories) on my mind. In other words, 'me' is a conglomeration of *all* my personal experiences - all of my memories.

'Me' is an inner world that can't be known by looking outside - it's not physical. 'Me' has to be deconstructed and will strongly resist that process, which it does for several reasons - including that it wants to survive, making the task intensely arduous - requiring our full attention. Consequently, we cling to our images and do our best to become 'someone' that confirms our existence - to play our chosen roles in this world (doctor, housewife, politician, accountant, etc.) to the best of our ability. Here's an example of what I mean. I may ask myself 'Who am I?' and the automatic answer would be

'Renée' but I know that's not who I am, so I question how that automatic answer came about. I answer 'Renée' because that's what I've been called all my life - that's the name people use when they refer to me - it's the lie that I've made true. It's the name I turn around to when I hear it and say 'Yes?', it's the name on identity documents and countless other places, it's where 'me' can be 'found', but it's not *me*. It's just a name I learnt to respond and pin memories to; for example, Renée likes 'this', doesn't like 'that' and belongs to a particular group, nation or class system. Over the years, the name Renée has been kneaded repeatedly until it was exactly the right texture and consistency to become what I've come to know as 'me'. This is how our characters are gradually formed as we become deeply conditioned to believe in the images, words and judgements we associate with them. These 'descriptions' become our memories and we pay just as much attention to them as we do the images, words and judgements others have formed about us; we're totally engrossed in our egos and the feedback we receive about them - our egos have made our bodies their home. Some of these memories are lies, some are truths and some are lies that we've made true. Have you ever thought about what it is that makes you 'you'?

~~~

This is a hard-going chapter and I promise you I won't be offended if you skip ahead to the next one, or even put the book down. For me however, it's my passion/purpose and I must continue to write it - at times, it all makes my head spin, but it's a feeling that urges me
~~~

on rather than pushes me back. No matter what we do to disguise the truth about ourselves or pretend that a truth doesn't exist, no matter how busy or distracted we keep ourselves so we don't have to think about these things, they'll *always* be there lurking and nagging in the background reminding us what frauds we are.

~~~

An actor can't *become* someone else, but he can play a role and this process requires a good memory. The actor has to learn to speak in the voice/accent of the character he wishes to portray, learning the character's mannerisms, thought processes, prejudices, body language and even what he likes to eat or drink. He must behave and look like the character - top hat, flat cap, weapons, costumes and other accessories - whatever he needs to be convincing. He has to absorb all this information and then the 'memories' can be accessed via thought - as soon as he needs them. To play a role well an actor must have the memories and thoughts of his character; he must *become* the character he wishes to play - effectively, becoming the character's ego. At the end of the play however, the actor drops the façade and returns to 'himself' once more. I'd suggest that the 'parts' of the actor and the character he plays could easily become intermingled as, when playing another role, it's inevitable that some memories must 'stick' - after all, these created our personalities to begin with.

An actor learns his part and replays it often during rehearsals and actual performances to such an extent that he may not even think about his lines or actions, as they
~~~

become second nature - an alter-ego. These memories are always accessible for him to recall and should he falter slightly, there are directors and other stage staff to prompt him. There's often a transition where an actor comes off stage and is still 'in character' - he's not yet fully returned to his own, particularly if he's played his role well. It's a bit like coming off the motorway; it takes a while to get used to driving slower again and it's easy to pick up speed without realising that we're driving over the speed limit. We've become so fully engrossed in the roles we play that we're unaware we're playing them - we can't see that we're made up of memories; the memories of the people who gave them to us - the memories we've cached. We're ingenious actors so it's no wonder we don't want to let go of our roles - our multiple 'me's.

Needless-to-say, I now appreciate why people don't like to think about these things. Delving into the mysterious or unknown can be frightening - so much so that we prefer to immerse ourselves in the many familiar distractions that society has to offer; entertainment, information, exercise, travel, work, fantasy and consumption. In particular, we immerse ourselves in future projects such as preparing adequately for our old age, a wedding, a birth or next year's holiday - *anything* but face the possibility of quietly thinking. I've lost count of the number of people who have told me they 'don't like to think', but they do it all the time; what they really mean is that they don't like to think below the surface. For some however, like me, there's no choice but to 'delve' - nothing has changed my life so much for the better than self-reflection and a firm commitment to 'unlearn' the lot. As I wrote in my introduction, the restlessness I feel calls me with some urgency - I'm more than happy to answer that call, wherever it may lead.

~~~

Our minds are so full of contaminants that we can't see - or conceive of - that which is pure; we also don't accept - or know - that our minds are contaminated at all. For whatever reason, our innocence has been diluted by conditioning, prejudices, ownership, polluted dreams and identities that can never belong to us - identities made up of the ideas and images that our senses have been, and still are, bombarded with from the moment of our birth. Most importantly, we adapt these images according to our perception of the environment we live in - how we've been and continue to be conditioned. Thought creates our images; mother cooking in the kitchen, father supporting the family, pink for girls and blue for boys are just a few of the more traditional ones and we carry these images into our future, which is also the past. The future being the past takes a while to get to grips with, but let's keep it simple - what can you think about for the future that hasn't come from past conditioning and therefore experience? Thought creates and maintains our beliefs, fears and wishes; thought controls us and thought interrupts any attempt by us to be free from it. We can't imagine a perfect world because we don't *live* in one and have seen only the ideas and imagined worlds of the media. Take for example the images and ideas in the film *The Time Machine*, based on H. G. Wells' book. Utopia wasn't all it seemed to
~~~

be; there was mischief going on behind the scenes - mischief that the passive population were oblivious to. Had the whole film been about happy people sitting by the river with everything they needed, we would've been bored stiff while watching it. Our interest however, is maintained and believability sustained when we add a little mystery regarding time, together with a few familiar character types and mischievous situations - we take a framework we like the sound of - like the *Garden of Eden* for example - and then fill in the blanks according to our conditioning.

Another reason we can't imagine a perfect world is because to do so means dismantling the one we're living in - letting go of what defines us - the idea of 'Me'. To dismantle what we 'know' to be true is tantamount to psychological suicide - no-one wants to live without their beloved identity and its various branches of inter-relationships; mother, brother, friend etc. To imagine a perfect world we must first face the horror and lies about the one we live in; we have to recognise the illusions and little-by-little, take them apart - it's necessary to erase *all* thoughts about who we think we are, before discovering that there's much more to us. We have to recognise that thought is memory - thought is the past and thoughts are what the world is made up of and influenced by - thought is confined and therefore *limited*. One difficulty in realising this is that we're left with no niche to belong to anymore; we're exposed, alone, naked in no-man's-land and way beyond our conditioned comfort zones - very few people are prepared to venture that far out of bounds. It's *not* an easy journey and we can't force ourselves to begin it; it begins when we want it to and not a moment before.

Another concept that's difficult to grasp is that we're 'One' - humanity. We can't be told that we're 'One' because we don't have the memories/thoughts that allow us to process the concept - it's alien to us. Our conditioned memories limit us to the barriers and borders that we've grown up with; nations, countries, tribes, colours and families - these all lend credence to separation rather than Oneness. We can only *realise* that we're 'One' for ourselves and the tendency is to ridicule anyone who tries to tell us otherwise, as they're 'threatening' our traditions. The problem however, isn't about 'threatening' traditions - it's about thinking on another frequency - it's about change and to change we have to be prepared to leave all the things we were doing before behind.

I digressed a little - thought is like that.

When we think, we tend to go by the marked footpath - the way we've always gone - our conditioned route. When we recognise and are willing to accept that our thoughts are *not* our own we then access something new - something eternal, sacred and immediate. To put thought into perspective we have to look closely, as best we can, at what it is. There are no thoughts - absolutely none - that haven't been given to us by society and that includes by our families. We've been taught by education and advertising to have thoughts about things; like 'happy families', relationships, 'success' and disaster; we've been shown so many models of these and through association with them, outline and fill in our lives, ambitions and dreams; these thoughts are from memory and formulaic - they're seriously flawed inasmuch as they can't deliver what they promise. A thought comes from a memory - it comes from our experiences. It would be very difficult, if not impossible, to locate our first thought - from our first experience - or to remember the discussions of our parents or nursing staff around us at the moment of our births:

- 'It's a boy.'
- 'He's perfect.'
- 'Let's call him Jack.'
- 'He weighs 7lbs.'

Without language how can a baby receive and process this information? I say without language, but I'd suggest it would be more accurate to say that he's unable to respond yet. We don't know if he's able to *understand* what we're saying - even if on some other level - but can't rule out the possibility and this would be a frustrating experience for the child if it were the case; we also can't rule out that thought may well begin in the womb. We can ask questions about our existence as we grow older, but the responses given to us can only come from the past. To elaborate a little more on this point, we get answers from reference books, from the media, from people we know or from our own memories - these answers are located in the past and there are a great many of them to amuse ourselves with. It's for this reason that searching for 'truth' on the outside is futile.

Quintessentially, there's something behind our memories and thoughts - something resistant to being conditioned yet at the same time, accepts this conditioning as the 'norm'. We can't see beyond this norm because we're conditioned not to; we must stay in line fearing consequences, should we choose to do otherwise. Yet there are times when we get to glimpse through the veil of conditioning - rather like getting a glimpse of the sun through heavy clouds; the same clouds that quickly cover it up again. Perhaps we convince ourselves that we never actually saw the sun - whereas we know we did, but choose to ignore any thoughts that tell us otherwise. We choose the thoughts and memories that bring us the most comfort and security. When I think of marmalade I think of 'marmalade on toast' and would venture that this is true for most people, but, for me to begin putting marmalade on jacket potatoes for example, could cause consternation for those familiar to me - raising not only eyebrows, but all sorts of questions regarding my 'sanity'. To act beyond our conditioning is *so* socially unacceptable that we bring pressure on those who do, to 'reform' themselves by stepping back into line - we prefer them to be like us because that doesn't threaten the *status quo*. New thoughts, that contradict the old, are unacceptable to the majority of us; we go to great lengths to upgrade everything in this world, except our minds - we resist this adaptation.

I'd suggest that we must have known - or had access to finding out - what we were doing here *before* we became so heavily indoctrinated, thus causing us to forget all about it - why else are we not encouraged to remember, discuss and study this topic; it's an important topic for every one of us, but instead of looking at it, we bury it beneath a great deal of unimportant diversionary nonsense. It's this nonsense that blocks all possible access points to that which is eternal. What's clear to me is that something existed *before* our characters were moulded - a predisposition. 'Me' is and continues to be a bundle of memories and thinking is the tool I use to access them. These memories are everything we're conscious of; for example, our names, addresses, professions, titles, opinions, fears, hates, histories, beliefs, rituals, sentiments and hopes. They're our stored experiences; they're the contents of our minds or if you will, the seeds from which our egos took root and flourished. We can only be free when we're free of thought and that's only possible in the Now as this is where we breach the limitations of thought itself and therefore, our fears - where there's no ego, space or time. If we try to stop thinking we can't; there are always thoughts keeping us busy and they come and go - at random - like confusing dreams, picked and collected from different periods of our lives that have nothing to do with where we are now. When we look closely at - or at least allocate a little of our precious time to the nature of *thought* then our lives can change significantly and in that process, the world becomes more magnificent and mysterious than we ever thought it could be. Memory then, is all we've absorbed - thought is playing back those memories. Thinking then, is a process by which we search through our databanks in search of those memories and assemble them according to our disposition. Where those memories lead us to and how much time we choose to linger with them is entirely up to us.

Taking Stock - A Perspective

The world doesn't care about us,
because we don't care about it.

To see the world in a different 'light' it's necessary to realise that life isn't like a film, book or soap opera. There are no choreographed fight scenes down our streets where no-one gets injured, no-one who wakes up in the mornings with their makeup intact, no 'lady in the red dress', no perfect figure, no spotless complexion, no spaceship hovering a few hundred feet above us and no fire-breathing dragons - above all, no superhero that's going to save us from ourselves; life just isn't like that. The world seen through the filters of the media is entirely different to the one we recognise in our society, yet fantasy is very much a part of our 'reality' and we accept it as such. Images - such as the above - are promoted heavily and their effect distorts perception and perspective, leading to feelings of inadequacy, powerlessness and apathy. Such feelings leave us prey to whatever society provides us with, so that we may seek 'perfection' by comparing ourselves to those who have 'it' and those who haven't. These images are controls by which we're steered towards illusions - like games or trends - where we can dream and become whatever we want to be. But they're not *our* dreams - they're manufactured 'junk food' - they're spam for our brains! The spell of these dreams is easily broken when we catch a glimpse of ourselves in a mirror or wake up in the mornings either alone, or perhaps next to a frog who failed to turn into a prince - no wonder we return to our more comfortable and acceptable illusions. While there's nothing wrong with doing this, if it gets us through the day, what if we could set ourselves free by looking at what's really happening - at how the world is being manipulated and how the majority of people have been drawn into an intricate 'spider's web' of distractions and illusions. Because many can't see that they're living in a controlled environment, it's understandable that they've no wish to break free from it.

So what?

If we've been attracted into a 'web' then it follows that something did the attracting; *what* that is isn't important - only that we submit and agree to live under its cloak of deceit. This leaves us feeling powerless because our power is in someone *else's* hands, by our choice. Multiply that power by the world's population and it becomes apparent how the world has become so unbalanced - the few have a great deal. We've become so locked into the pull of desire, fear, success, failure, protection and separation that we actually believe one human being is more powerful than another - that they've an advantage over us, perhaps by having been born in the right place at the right time. This isn't the case; however, we believe it to be true and give other people the authority to control the lives of ourselves and our children. Perhaps you can't see this, but then I invite you to think about who decides when to invade another country, who pays for it and who's told that it's in the interest of *our* safety; isn't it more in the interests of those who want to continue being in control? Those same people make up our laws, educate our children, judge others, control our media, earn huge salaries and through 'VIP status' or 'diplomatic immunity' are given exemption from taking responsibility for their actions - they don't subject themselves to the laws they impose on us. Most importantly, think about who voted them into office on a wave of enthusiasm encouraged by the media and our 'fed-up-ness' with things the way they are - unhindered by the knowledge that *nothing* is going to change for the better. For every cause and effect there are consequences - there'll always be a price to pay for our apathy and reliance on our various elected 'authorities'.

Who are the authorities? We are. There's no real domination or submission, there's simply an imbalance, kept in place by our fears. Each one of us is different inasmuch as we were born into different cultural environments - environments that existed *before* our 'birth'. Environments created to maintain separation in such a way that the system we created grows stronger and more violent as that division continues; like us, it began with the first division of a 'cell' and has continued exponentially ever since. So why do we follow the laws of others? That's a *very* good question and needs meditating on, but mostly because there *are* laws and, even though some are illogical, we're conditioned to obey them - 'Simple Simon' says, and we do. The trouble with laws is that we become dependent on them to tell us what we can and can't do, and then complain when these laws are enforced - we've lost our ability to filter out the nonsense. We want other people to submit to these laws, even when we don't always obey them ourselves - we can be rather bossy and superior; the 'artful' bend these laws to suit their own agendas. Why do we have laws at all? That's a good question too. We have laws because we're irresponsible and selfish - it's that simple. For example, we need speed limits because we speed and put others at risk when we're doing it. A concept that's unfamiliar to many is that, in some cases, the laws really *are* for our protection - too often from ourselves. However, the laws are created - and enforced - by the same sickness of mind that made the need for them necessary, so what we get is more disorder and no justice. The more we behave 'badly', the more new laws will be created; for example, litter laws are necessary *only* because we throw our litter onto pavements and driving laws, because we drive recklessly and inconsiderately. We don't *need* the laws at all. What we need is to take responsibility - to allow ourselves to evolve in a way that widens our perspective, so we see that the way we behave has an effect on everything and everyone around us, and to *care* about that. If we're to evolve, psychologically, then we must become a law unto ourselves - for the *good* of mankind, not the detriment; if we choose not to - yes, it *is* a choice - then our prospects are rather bleak.

~~~

As individuals, can we do anything about what's happening all over the world? No! There's nothing we can do. That statement should have the effect of taking
~~~

a heavy weight off our minds but it doesn't; it leaves us feeling apathetic and more powerless than ever. The world outside of our own perspective can't be changed by us personally. *Everyone* has to change - to stop doing whatever they're doing and take stock, rather than examine the world as 'armchair activists' focused on the large variety of world issues our minds are constantly directed towards. Bearing this in mind we know the world's population is not going to have that enviable 'light bulb' moment at the same time, so we do what we've always done - wait for someone or something to flick the switch for us - maybe by divine intervention or a superhero; who knows? The problem is that we don't see the whole picture, but only snippets. By way of illustration, the job of one person in this world may be to stamp out a metal shape and another's, somewhere else in the world, is to form that shape in to a part that gets sent on elsewhere to be attached to a frame of some sort. None of these workers know or care what's being constructed, how other members of the team are contributing towards it, or what its ultimate purpose is. We care only for the money we receive in our wage packets, so that we're able to pay our ever increasing bills, feed our families, accumulate 'more' and continue to heedlessly consume our world.

~~~

When the sky and outer space are beyond our reach and our ability to 'leave the planet' is limited to being up in one of our various flying machines - with the inevitable return to earth - everything can feel a little
~~~

hopeless. We hear a great deal of bad news - every day - and sometimes even good news can feel 'bad', if it leaves us feeling frustrated or envious. Consequently, in 'powerless mode', we become engrossed in the various diversions provided for us - be it work or play - as they give the illusion of being in control while we're having a 'good time' or trying to 'make something of ourselves'. We temporarily forget about - or rather put to the back of our minds - all the things we're dissatisfied with - we don't like to think about them. We prefer the illusion of being in control, because we're uncomfortable with the noise of our thoughts when everything around us is silent - when we're alone. We're more comfortable living with the noise and chaos of society; when the world is screaming at us, *we* don't have to scream at it.

Certainly the diversions we're surrounded by can leave us entertained and often amused, but they also leave us feeling undervalued, insignificant and ignored - we don't like to feel that way. These diversions also encourage us to 'join in' so we become actors, online chefs, exhibitionists and comedians for example - hoping for likes, followers and approval; we look for something or someone to acknowledge and take notice of our very existence, but it's all rather cliché and the vast majority of us remain invisible, despite our masks of anticipated/ achieved popularity or fame. We take whatever we can get, but underneath there's a scream, a sorrow and a person who knows they're effectively banging their head against a brick wall - a person who's lost in this world, just like the rest of us.

It sounds hopeless doesn't it, but I invite you to think about whose voice is telling you that? Isn't it the voice of the ego that's 'quite comfortable as it is' and has no intention of exerting itself in order to change? We've been given the ability to find meaning in our lives - to work out what we're doing here and to have compassion for each other. We hear that distant voice - behind the ego - that we so often ignore in favour of our desires and comforts. We tune it out, rather like a television or radio station, to prevent the cross talk interfering with our chosen frequency and so that we can't hear anything else, we turn up the volume. If we *really* want to change we need to tune in to the voice we ignore and see the ego for what it is - a creation of our mind. If we don't - if we remain between 'stations' - then all we'll ever hear is white noise. Be aware that the mind is a clever trickster and offers us any number of 'good reasons' to remain as we are - it doesn't want us to change frequency by giving up its creation or allowing us a vision of a better world. The mind is our prison and its walls have been continuously reinforced for a long, long time. I'm not going to tell you that it's easy to free ourselves from within these walls, because that wouldn't be true. I can however, assure you that changing ourselves changes the way we see the world and though that can be a herculean task, it's worth the effort - *if* we don't give up. During the course of our lifetimes we've suffered many disappointments and setbacks; we've also been discouraged from doing 'our own thing' unless it suits the agenda of society. For these reasons we don't expect or believe that anything positive will or can take place in our lives - *that's* what I mean by giving up.

~~~

A play begins when the curtains open and ends when they close again; our lives begin when we're born, and end when our eyes close for the last time. We fear the end, but not what we put between it and the beginning; we don't give this much intelligent thought at all. Our lives are important enough for us to be here, so they should also be important enough for us to participate in the world in a meaningful and responsible way, as opposed to being an audience for those who wish to control us, as though we'd somehow drawn the 'short straw' on who takes charge. We feel obliged and accept unquestioningly living in *their* world, rather than creating our own. It doesn't matter what circumstances we're born
~~~

into. What matters is how our *minds* develop and how we lift ourselves out of fear, dependence, helplessness, self-pity and despair.

Humanity needs a 'sea change', a change of mindset, and that mindset changes a little each time one of us puts our 'weapons' down; it isn't an *en masse* overnight process. By weapons, I don't just mean guns; I also mean gossip, jealousy, envy, hatred, spite, judgement, anger and snobbery - wielded by over-inflated egos. When we raise our consciousness and see the bigger picture, it isn't possible to behave in a destructive or inconsiderate manner. I'd suggest that we're not here to 'succeed' in this world; we're not here to win a war; we're here to evolve and to transform ourselves - psychologically. We're here to raise the level of our consciousness and right now - for the majority - it's being lowered by, amongst other things, our encouraged need to 'out-do' each other. Any form of competition is separation; if we meet, you may want to show me what you do and how you do it so much better than I can, and I may wish to show you the same thing from my perspective. This situation results in competitiveness and comparison - it may also get us the approval, admiration, recognition and acceptance that we all seek, but there are consequences. When we strive to become Number One, we're striving for someone else not to be good enough; when we strive to 'have' we strive for someone else to 'have not'.

No-one cares about us more than we do. We're more than a little interested in *ourselves* and for this reason we're not very good at seeing perspective, if it doesn't agree with our own. If we have a problem then that problem is as big - if not bigger - than the world and to all intents and purposes, we're alone with it. At our lowest point, like when we lose our job or a relationship ends, our lives feel like they've come to an end and nothing can ease our mind or make us feel better.

As far as we're concerned, in situations such as these, the rest of the world doesn't exist as no-one understands the urgency of our situation with the same intensity that we do, neither will they give it priority. Sure, we can discuss our problems with friends or even acquaintances, but mostly - like us - they'll be more concerned with their own and more importantly, they really can't help us by bringing back what we've 'lost' - they can only console us and what practical use is that consolation. The world can support us when things get tough and it may genuinely try to help, but it can't solve our problems, live our lives for us or give them meaning. No matter how busy our social life is - real or virtual - we're each of us entirely alone with our thoughts and have an agenda seen *only* from our *own* perspective - our true intentions are rarely aired.

Between the covers of birth and death we write our unique stories - mostly tragic or full of missed opportunities and possibilities, rather than 'happy ever after' endings. Is it any wonder then, that our literature and other media are full of those same horrors, reflecting, reinforcing and magnifying them - after all, *we* are the writers of it. It's not that we're 'bad' inside, we just want someone else to show us the way, to solve our problems *for* us, so that we no longer have to be afraid and then we'll be happy - a 'when my boat comes in' mentality. As I mentioned earlier, life just isn't like that and we're lazy when it comes to doing things that are good for us; we also want someone to follow - someone to go first, for them to take the risks thereby clearing our path - a sort of guarantee that we won't stumble, fall or set off any 'explosions'. Ironically, we also want to be followed in some way - we're both sheep and shepherd. This is very much part of the nature of our world today, as is profoundly evident on our social media 'friends' and 'follow' lists. We can accept life as it is, as many prefer to do, or stop and take stock - to examine well our situation and overcome the belief that we can't change ourselves. We can start writing a new chapter any time we want to; all that's needed is a change of perspective - a change that happens by itself when we look at the whole picture.

Sometimes discerning what's happening is just a question of changing our perspective. If for example. there's a 1 in 100 chance of winning the lottery, we get more of an idea about what that means when we see that there's a 99 in 100 chance of losing. If the lottery were advertised this way we wouldn't buy tickets. When we turn things around they'll look very different. However, we're taught to think about the odds of *winning* and the word sticks. We're attached to 'hope' and getting 'lucky' - we choose these, even though we know it's futile. We can't see the truth about our world whilst arguing against it. For example, we choose to use the word 'winning' as opposed to 'losing', because no one wants to hear about losing, despite - in the case of the lottery - it being the more likely outcome.

~~~

Think about which characters would get the most exposure if you decided to put your story onto paper; in other words, who dominates your thoughts and by definition, your life. In my case it was my father, and an autobiography I drafted was nothing more than a sob story in which he played the 'starring role'. I came to realise that I was nothing more than an extra in my own life story with no lines of my own - therefore, I burnt it, because my father was starring in *my* life instead of me. Once I realised this, it became unacceptable to continue
~~~

giving him so much space in *my* mind - it wasn't good for me. We have to realise that we're strange, very strange, and that we do the craziest things; for example, going on a diet and perhaps rewarding ourselves once a week for the effort we made, with something that *isn't* good for us - we call it a 'treat'. We rarely have our own best interests at heart. If we make little efforts to change the way we think and behave, then the world we see will begin to change for the better and we'll start to 'know ourselves' in a whole new and intelligent way - if we up the ante, it'll change much faster.

It's important not to see ourselves as victims of the authorities - like us, they're an audience. They watch us for change just as we watch them, and through statistics and observation they know how to keep us occupied and entertained. They give us what we want - someone else to take responsibility, and we give them what they want - 'power' and 'control'. Our feedback through various channels, informs the authorities about the mood of the general public and our own genius creates new fads and technological advances to placate us, but only with what we're able to absorb at the time. In other words, as long as we want to play games then games are what we'll create. Our games, phones and computers get frequent 'updates', but our minds don't; we can only upgrade that ourselves - yes, we can 'upgrade' it - and that can't happen as long as we allow our minds to continuously be infected by the various viral activities of society. There's a big difference between being controlled by society's wishes for us, and really being in control ourselves. It's that frequency thing again; when we're ready to change then it'll happen and not a moment before; until then we must continue to live under the parental arm and control of the society we created - it's there both for our protection and destruction and will be, for as long as we choose not to take responsibility for ourselves. It's a symbiotic relationship and it'll remain that way, until we take our power back. The authorities have no power without our compliance. It's our power that not only drives, but strengthens and advances the system - without that power we're greatly weakened. To vastly simplify this point; our compliance is the only power our elected authorities have - they'll hold on to it, until we're ready and responsible enough to handle it ourselves.

Relationships

*As we climb a mountain, the valley
becomes clearer and clearer.*

During the course of our lifetime, we encounter many different people - some from our own culture and others from significantly different ones. Some of these encounters may last for just a split second - as with passers-by - and sometimes we establish relationships for a lifetime. There are people who we meet at the moment of their birth and others at the moment of their death. Stranger, are the relationships that only take place in our imaginations, such as with a 'celebrity' or a character in a book or film. No matter what the type of meeting, we 'eye up' and categorise each other based on our conditioned images, prejudices and fears - always aware of any possible threat to our 'stability' and in particular to our 'safety' - we're *en garde*. We're humanity - the *human* family - but we've been divided into nations, colours, religions, age groups, classes, levels of education, the Smiths and the Jones's. It's these divisions that cause all of our problems as we strive to fulfil our own agendas - on our own 'side', behind our own 'flag' and these are our first priority; we tend to offer only 'spare change' for anything else. Regardless of the conditions under which we meet - because of the images that divide us - we can never fully know anyone, unless we're willing to drop all conditioned responses, to see our extended 'family' through unfettered eyes.

Relationships are complex and if we're honest, few of us welcome so-called 'outsiders' into our lives or speak to them on an equal footing - an outsider, being someone who doesn't fit into our accepted culturally-conditioned environment. Such outsiders have had different experiences to our own - some better, some worse, and it's through our biased experiences and adopted opinions that we judge them. These judgements are often based on propaganda spread by the media, such as about immigrants waiting to enter 'our' country; we worry that they'll drain us of our resources when in truth it's more likely that we've drained them of theirs, which is why they seek our help now. Other outsiders are those we fleetingly pass by without any real contact; for example, once, whilst driving, I caught sight of a lorry coming my way and as we passed by each other I saw the driver's face. I remember thinking that I'd never know who the man was; I'd never know how he's suffered, what he's going through now, where he's going, where he came from, or whether he has similar thoughts as he passes other people by. We generally encounter people every day of our lives and most of them we don't give a second thought to; however, our worlds *do* meet - albeit briefly. For example:

- Passively, as when standing in a queue.
- Actively, when greeting a colleague or client.
- Peacefully, at mutually agreeable venues
- Suspiciously, when meeting for the first time.
- Hopefully, when noticing a beneficial opportunity.
- Violently, to one degree or another, such as when or being 'pushed and shoved' through a crowd.

When meeting people for the first time we pigeon hole them into categories; such as, threat, naïve, 'keep at a distance', attractive, 'useful person to know' or 'avoid at all costs'; there are far too many to list and some of these are physical, some psychological, but *all* of our scrutinised categories and judgements are based on our past experiences. We euphemistically call this 'summing someone up', but when we do that we could miss a magic moment or a kindness that could result from such a chance encounter, simply because we look for confirmation of our judgement, which can obscure anything to the contrary. We brush shoulders in one way or another with other people during our daily lives, never noticing them, never knowing them and if we're honest, never really caring. We miss out on so many opportunities to make a difference when we fail to notice the world around us - when we're in 'I' 'Me' 'My' mode.

Circumstantial relationships are common and given little thought. We're quick to judge people if they're connected to someone we once knew; for example, the new girlfriend of an ex-boyfriend we feel resentment towards. No matter who our 'ex' dates, we'd likely hate them on first sight if we still have feelings for him; more likely we'd dislike them even before we met as jealousy and pride kick in. If however, we were to meet the same girl under different circumstances - like at a party - we'd probably get on rather well; after all, we must have something in common to have attracted the same man. So many of our mutually beneficial relationships are shallow, and reciprocal only if we're on the same 'team' such as in schools, sports, sects or competing businesses; should someone change allegiance, then our feelings towards them become more or less favourable than they were before - our friend then becomes our enemy or our enemy our friend - raising the question what exactly is it we require of someone in order to accept them as a friend. We've probably all been in relationships where we're expected to drop someone simply because our 'best friend' has fallen out with them - many comply with this demand; we miss out on so much when we allow ourselves to be divided by circumstance. There's also a dark side to circumstantial relationships where we're manipulated - or manipulate - as a means to an end and these are the most destructive of relationships as they invoke mistrust, betrayal and the like - they're far more common than most people would like to admit. Personal and business relationships are often based on an 'agreement' whereby as long as each person is doing what the other one wants things run smoothly; questioning in such a relationship can start sparks flying and bring the relationship to a swift end; for example, when a child disagrees with a parent, or an employee with his boss; when two sticks are rubbed together they'll produce a fire.

Families create the most complicated of relationships and based on current knowledge, we don't choose which family to become a part of. The word 'family' implies closeness, but we know that most families are anything but. If we look at humanity as a whole it's possible to see why that is - family members are just as divided as anyone else and only a surname (a tag or a label) connects them. Being a family is really just another form of separation - a further division - a division from everyone else. The ethnocentric nature of families demand that they stick together no matter what - because of this, the blood bond is difficult to break away from or to do without. It would cause us more loneliness than ever *not* to be a part of a family - we can't just leave one and join another; an adopted family member will always remain just that, no matter how much affection may be felt for them - often apparent in moments of high dudgeon. In reality, families are divided amongst themselves and each member has their own strong views. No matter how one particular view may be frowned upon or discouraged by other family members, it *can't* be changed or destroyed and will smoulder in our hearts until we're able, or decide to go our own way - perhaps as the 'black sheep', perhaps on a 'guilt trip' for standing up for ourselves instead of living with a loyalty that's one-sided. If we turn our backs on our own beliefs, we can end up remaining bitter for the rest of our lives - a bitterness that ferments and is detrimental only to ourselves. What can we do if we find ourselves in this position? I can only give you the benefit of my experience, which involved waiting until I was *legally* and *mentally* old enough to make my own decisions (wisely or not), yet all the while, observing the situation and learning from it; in particular, learning that I could only change myself, *never* others - despite the apparent 'unfairness' and 'injustice' of it all. This understanding was key to my letting go, though it took many years and much strife for me to come to terms with.

A married couple will often stay together, even if their relationship is destructive, for a variety of reasons including for the 'benefit' of the children, yet many choose to divorce; when this happens we tend to leave a trail of victims behind. Divorce is not just the separation of two people who no longer get along - any children are affected by the division and also the relatives and friends of the two families that were forged together when the marriage took place. On divorce, members of the family become polarised, based on who they 'supported' before the marriage - things that were once considered 'ours' now become 'yours' and 'mine', if they're not broken in the battle, and here I'm not only referring to material belongings. As with friendships, a relationship with a family can be dependent on whose side we're on and if that includes the separation of children from one of their parents or their grandparents, then that's what we'll work to bring about - allowing personal feelings, pride and judgment to take precedence over kindness or the welfare and consideration of others.

Somewhere along the line we've gone horribly wrong in our ideas about what it means to be a family. Consider this. We create new families, not just for biological reasons, but also and often foremost by reason of conditioned sentimentality - such as romance - and a need for security in a society that encourages us to be dependent on it. We search for our 'happy ever after' home because we feel lost, need somewhere to belong, somewhere we feel safe, and a 'family' relationship is one of the ways in which we feel this; a career away from a family environment is another, but *both* are illusions - both create continuity of what we're seeking security from. There's something status-hugging about getting married and starting a family; we construct life-size doll's houses and fill them with everything we can get into them including children, gadgets, furniture, toys etc. - some of us decide we'd be better off living alone. Having attained these 'ideals' we spend our lives striving to maintain the *status quo* often putting our children into some form of 'day care' - including schools - in order to do that. This is the situation and example that we pass on to our children, which can never change anything in the world for the better; it's frustrating and leads to further painful division - often a division between parents and their children causing bitterness and resentment. At some point, we're going to have to make sense of the increasing disruption going on in the world - we can do that by first seeing what's going on in our *own*.

When the whole of anything is divided it no longer *seems* to be complete; though that *is* stating the obvious, it's something that doesn't occur to many people. Humanity has been mischievously fractured by an unstable mind (*our* mind) and the cracks have been filled with conflict with all its attendant hatred, sorrow, violence and fear, forming a mosaic that has some semblance of One - but it's a rather ugly and heavily conditioned One - having the effect of further dividing people. Humanity is *still* complete - it can never be anything else - *but*, it's a 'complete mess'! We need to clean up our act by raking out that hard and inflexible filling and replacing it with love - a love that will draw the pieces together rather than keeping them apart. We also need to pay attention to our relationships and see them for what they are, then and only then can compassion and empathy flourish in our society. As long as we're slaves to a society that persists in driving us into situations that cause further instability in the world, we'll remain as we are, as we've been for a *very* long time - searching for a place where we can live in peace without fear of disruption - searching for our home, not in outer space, but in our hearts.

Too often missing from our relationships - I'd suggest *most* of the time - is selflessness. No matter how much we think we're considering the thoughts and feelings of another person, it's hard to remove the ego from our interactions. Being selfless doesn't come easy; there's always that internal accountant trying to balance the books - scrutinising any payment that doesn't promise some sort of return. In the end, we place relationships in the debtor's journal awaiting a repayment; for example, doing a favour for someone and thinking 'they owe me', even if we try to push that thought away. We need to make the accountant redundant and not refill the position - though our ego will put forward suitable replacements for consideration.

When we learn to 'give' with no thought of a return we develop the most complete and important relationship we can ever have. This is the relationship we must forge with ourselves, and *this* is the relationship we put up the most resistance to 'having'; this is the *only* relationship in which we can ever find peace - the relationship in which we're at ease and the relationship in which the ego can't dominate. From our births to our deaths we spend *every* second with ourselves - awake and asleep - on holiday or not - and *every* one of them is precious; we can never be away from ourselves - our true nature - no matter how high a wall we build to keep it hidden. Death can come to any one of us at any moment without prior warning and few are prepared for it - most are still grasping for the things we *can't* keep; only a few have gone into themselves with the dedication required to discover their 'root' - a root from which we can never be torn. Our journey and the state of mind we're in when we die *is* important - the state of our body is not. Although some people have buried this realisation deeper than others, no matter how much we deny it, no matter how many arguments we create to avoid seeing the truth, no matter how much we torture ourselves with inner debates on matters such as 'life after death' in whatever form we choose to imagine, we *know* our lives have purpose and meaning *now* - this knowledge is innate!

The Control Conundrum

*There's no control without consent
and no consent without control.*

When you're next out and about take a look at a newspaper stand - you'll find there's *nothing* on it that inspires or motivates, nothing life-changing and nothing that's not been seen before. The newspaper headlines grind at our emotions, fill us with anxiety, anger, envy, outrage, fear and guilt sending us further into our shells, yet we continue to buy them in order to 'keep up-to-date' with what's going on in the world - it's expected of us and we like doing it. The headlines, emblazoned on the front pages, are generally about attacks, robberies, murders, corruption, drugs, missing children, injustice and badly behaving 'celebrities' of one sort or another - different faces, ages or backgrounds, but essentially the same old fear-inducing stories - there's no balance. Someone, somewhere wants to keep us in a state of anxiety; why don't we question that? Whether we're aware of it or not we *are* influenced by these front pages as we scan over them - they leave us feeling deflated and powerless to change anything and to compound this, we feel compelled to wallow in the *full* story. Just who is in control of this situation?

The flood of negative information from newspaper headlines, advertisements and countless other media -

impossible to entirely avoid - is unknowingly absorbed, too often leaving us with an inexplicable background feeling of impending doom. Avert our eyes from the headlines and we'll find 'feel good' diversions such as hobby, holiday, property, car, pet, fashion and glamour magazines, puzzle books, confectionery, fizzy drinks and sandwiches; these are some of the antidotes we happily turn to - putting us 'back in control', or so we believe, but they're there for the purpose of igniting our desires, consoling and distracting us; they temporarily make us feel better and like other 'pain killers' it's only a matter of time before we require another dose. It's in our nature to want to be in control of our lives, in any way that we can; however, we're being ingeniously directed - under assault - at *every* turn.

There's another pervasive diversion from reality and that's gaming. We're bombarded - on our various devices - with notifications of someone's high score, someone's latest post, invitations to play etc. - the temptation to 'play' can be irresistible. We lose ourselves in gaming worlds because we're unable to comprehend or face the horrors of our own. Whether or not we like them, whether or not we play them, gaming is now a huge part of our world. Games fully absorb us into them while we're playing; they give us a feeling of being in control, a feeling that evaporates when we're away from our screens or virtual reality headsets; because of this, these games *are* addictive - we're far too quick to deny this fact. When we shoot at or kill other players, rob banks, drop bombs or whatever we do in these games we can't be arrested, tried or convicted - we get away scot-free.

We take risks while participating in the games, knowing that we can't be harmed in any way - risks we wouldn't take in 'real life - there are no injuries, no deaths and no responsibilities. Shooting at someone in a game in today's world is equivalent to knocking over a tin soldier, or playing 'cowboys and Indians' in 'times gone by'. We can choose to behave violently, destroy the world and set ourselves up as heroes or villains without any apparent consequences. Consequences or not, violence is the act we're committing whether in real life or the gaming world; the majority of these games *are* violent in one way or another - increasingly gratuitous - as, inevitably, are our thoughts when we play them.

In a world we appear to have no control over it's no wonder we immerse ourselves in these fantasies - fantasies that give us, albeit an illusion, the feeling of being in control. We become so immersed in these games that we forget what time it is, whether or not we're hungry, all about the environment our body exists in and the people we share that environment with; gaming is an *out-of-body* experience - it's escapism. When our concentration is interrupted we get irritated - sometimes angry - out of all proportion, even if the call is to come down for a meal. When away from our screens for longer periods of time all we can think of is getting back to the game. We don't want to be pulled out of our fantasies back into the 'reality' that we're rejecting. I've seen extreme examples of this where nothing matters except 'The Game', not even food, hygiene or sleep; the games further divide those who are playing them from those who don't - often destroying personal or business relationships. It becomes apparent, when you take a step back and really look at the world, that it's awash with games of one sort or another; sporting, digital, shows, lotteries and countless other forms of games, including the mind games we play with ourselves and each other. There are consequences to this state of affairs. While we're busy in the playground our world, is being destroyed all around us and people everywhere are suffering. Instead of being in control of our world, we're controlled by the world of games. We're advancing technologically, but not physically (so many are sick in our world) or spiritually (so many have no hope left) or psychologically (we can no longer think for ourselves) and therefore, have no control over our lives. While we're influenced and controlled by these reality-altering games, instead of considering our existence and helping mankind out of its decline, our lives have no worthwhile meaning or value. Our life-clock however, is still ticking away as a reminder that our time here is passing.

~~~

Recognising what we can and can't change in society is an important part of changing ourselves and consequently, our world. Changing ourselves is a choice - do it or don't. If we decide to change then with that decision comes freedom from the diversions of those who wish to maintain the *status quo*, by appealing to and controlling our desire for consolation and distraction from our pains; consolation and distractions that generally aren't good for our physical *or* mental health - which is just one reason why we lead such unhealthy and
~~~

stressful lives - leaving ourselves little time or inclination to make any kind of life-changing decisions. Imagine a film scene where someone has suffered a shock of some kind; in most cases are they not offered a sedative, cigarette or alcoholic drink to calm themselves? We're influenced by this suggestion and reach for drugs, alcohol, cigarettes or food when we need support, but they never support us; they provide an unhealthy distraction as we temporarily put our woes to one side - our sorrows can be suppressed, but they can't be drowned. When we reach for these distractions it's *us* who are in control of our actions, *us* who decide to bury our problems by not thinking about and elevating ourselves above entrapment; this is submitting ourselves to the control of others in a society that prefers us not to think at all; we willingly put our lives, and responsibility for them, in the hands of others. Paradoxically, the person who is being controlled is the one in control - being controlled is a choice. We're not naturally 'controllees', but take on the 'role' when we're afraid of possible repercussions and also when it's beneficial to us. Control - or rather authority over our actions - *has* never and *can* never been removed from us.

So much of the world, as portrayed, is out of our control and the most stable position for an individual to be in, is that of 'observer' - otherwise all we do is 'chase our tails'; the world is so out of control that no-one can possibly keep up with it. One piece of information conflicts with another and one of the greatest indicators of this is in our software 'updates'. When programs on my computer upgrade, others have to keep up with them or they don't function correctly anymore; for example, when our computer operating systems are updated - other programs may have to change with it or they become out-of-date and consequently, incompatible. My computer is always whirling away in the background updating something or another and this updating significantly slows down whatever I'm doing at the time - sometimes bringing it to a grinding halt, unless I make a decision to disconnect from the Internet and then my time is under my control. The same applies to our mobile phones. When I switch mine on in the mornings, more often than not it wants to update several applications to 'improve' my 'user experience' - this morning there were ten, but I experienced no improvement whatsoever. If we *don't* click in a box 'agreeing' to the update, then we may not be able to use the application and as many applications are interconnected this can cause operating problems - we've no control over this situation except to make a choice 'to agree' or 'not agree' in which case the application - and possibly others - won't function? No wonder it's so difficult to get off the 'wheel' of upgrades, upgrades and yet *more* upgrades - for everything but our minds. Like the programs that won't work without changes, neither will we; we have to get off the wheel. In the world we're creating, the need for money and possessions now far outweigh the need for intelligence, compassion or love for each other.

If we choose to abstain from keeping 'up-to-date', by distancing ourselves from 'current affairs' and spending our time away from the chaos, then we're largely seen as not caring about what's going on in the world, which in most cases couldn't be further from the truth.

Choosing not to swim in dirty water doesn't mean we don't care that it's dirty - it means that we prefer it to be clean. This action is not a slant against those who choose to remain as they are; it's a decision to remove ourselves from an unhealthy environment and take back control of our own lives, as far as is possible, without outside influence; it's a personal decision not to live in fear anymore - no matter what. It's also a firm decision to do anything we can to 'enquire' into the questions 'Who am I?' and 'What am I doing here?' even if the answers can't be fully understood during our lifetime. If our decision is in earnest, then the urge to change is so powerful that *nothing* can divert us.

~~~

Beneath the surface we're in full control of our own lives making choices every day; such as, what channel to watch, turn left or right, go to work or choose whether or not to finish reading a book; we make hundreds - if not thousands - of decisions every day without being aware that we're making them. Each choice we make produces a different effect on our lives; for example, the moment we choose to step into a road can result in us safely crossing it, serious injury, or even our death. We 'conduct' our lives *day-to-day* regardless of our circumstances or physical bodies; even from a hospital bed we can still smile - it's our energy that counts. We're *alive.* As long as we're alive, like 'a live wire', we're not disconnected from the energy that runs through us, but we *can* choose in which direction that energy flows and whether or not to suppress it. We can disconnect from our sorrows and pains and re-connect to what we've ignored for so long; what lies beneath our various masks - our fundamental nature, which is good. We can *choose* to be directed and follow the crowd, or to direct ourselves - following our own path. Our lives are full of contradiction and when it comes to talking about control there's more contradiction than ever. 'The control conundrum' is, who, if anybody, is in control of our lives? Ironically, there *is* no actual control - only the
~~~

effects of the choices we make based on the influences we're surrounded by.

Endurance

*Endurance is the strength to cope with a
hardship in whatever form it presents itself.*

Whatever age you are, whatever your character, skin colour, no matter what the condition of your health and regardless of whether you smoke, drink alcohol, eat junk food or not; regardless of whether you have tattoos, qualifications or have lost one or even all of your limbs - here you are reading this sentence; you've made it through *all* your problems and every one of those moments you believed you *couldn't* go on any longer - those moments when you wanted the ground beneath your feet to split open and swallow you up, burying you forever as your world came to a heart-breaking end. Every one of us has survived what we thought we couldn't, and that says a lot about the resolve of the human race to endure whatever's put in front of it, and about our resilience and ability to come back stronger than ever. Brilliant, aren't we? However, like all thoughts that I allow to seed there's more to endurance than that.

The 1980's Japanese show 'Endurance' holds the title in *The Guinness Book of Records* as the 'Most Extreme Game Show'. I don't need to go into examples of the rounds, but to win this show contestants push themselves to their limits by *volunteering* to suffer exquisite pain, degradation and humiliation, and, from the expressions on their faces - they love every minute of it; however, it's not just the contestants who love these shows but the audience too - without a show there's nothing for an audience to see and without an audience, there's not much point in putting on a show. As an audience, our minds put us in more or less the same mental state as the contestants whilst in reality, we're sitting on the edge of our seats peeping through our fingers or curling our toes, as we pick up on the energy and revel in the 'courage' of the contestants to endure what we (as virtual contestants) quite possibly couldn't. If we choose to sit on a throne of momentary 'stardom', which is what we get from participating in a television game show, a throne of self-delusion or any other throne then that's what we'll do - no matter what hardships we may have to endure whilst sitting on it. We have a tendency to want to prove ourselves *to ourselves* by pushing our limits of tolerance and that manifests itself in various forms of suffering; we'll put ourselves through a lot in order to fit into society. We endure - we always have!

Our lives have much in common with this Japanese game show, in that we volunteer to endure suffering - to one degree or another - in exchange for 'prizes' in much the same way; these prizes are not necessarily tangible and could be anything from a medal to approbation. We go to great pains keeping up appearances for our neighbours, colleagues, acquaintances, family or friends - necessary when we live in a way that requires us to have so many complicated inter-relationships. In most cases, we can't reveal our nature to everyone we know, as we behave in a different way with each of them. To an employer we behave in a way that's acceptable to him in order to take home a salary - our 'prize'; it's the *price* we're willing to endure in order to have a nice home with all the related 'trimmings'. In most cases, we wouldn't want to keep our jobs if it weren't for the fact that we need a salary to pay our bills; generally, we don't work for the love of the job but out of necessity - it's an investment. We can do the same thing with relationships; I know people who have remained in very stressful situations simply because they don't want to divide their home or give up the income and comfort that they've built up over the years - so they endure the misery in order to hold onto their possessions and comforts - very few are able to break away from a situation like this.

One of the problems with endurance is that once we pass our chosen targets, we set ourselves further ones; humans like to push far and beyond the limits they have surpassed. Imagine if you will, someone who goes to the gym for the purpose of building muscles; the extreme of them will never have enough 'bulk' for their liking, and so end up looking 'deformed' in the most horrible way - it's self-inflicted. We talk about space, reaching for the moon, perhaps Mars, setting ourselves targets and then we'll want to go further - no distance will ever be far enough to satisfy us. The issue here is desire - a desire to surpass and as always with humans that results in competition, as the only thing we can really try to surpass is each other; the muscles are needed to be stronger than someone else, the space travel because we want to 'get there' before anyone else, and of course money - we'll never have enough of that. At this point

I'm reminded of the old adage 'give them an inch and they'll take a mile'. We will endure - and cause others to endure - a great deal to achieve our goals.

We treat our bodies as though they were crash test dummies - testing them quite often to destruction. We starve them, overfeed them, poison them with alcohol and tobacco, eat over-processed modified 'food', pollute our vital air and water, and take drugs for entertainment; we're making ourselves *and* our planet ill and refuse to see that it's all self-induced; we've emotionally disconnected from what we're doing and the consequences of it. But, unlike crash test dummies our bodies aren't replaceable and we have to endure the results of our 'dare devil' activities. How much will we agree to endure before we tap into our intelligence and say 'enough is *enough*' instead of 'bring it on'? If it's still going on and getting worse, which it is, then we're pretty much okay with what's happening and don't want it to stop - at the very least, we don't want to do anything that will cause it to stop. We tend to go through life as willing packhorses ladened down with unnecessary loads. We *could* shed our load and walk away from it, but with that shedding comes the loss of a certain perverse status that we're unwilling (*not* unable) to give up - so we 'dutifully' endure whatever's put on us to keep that status going.

By now I expect some people are thinking about the endurance of an illness we can do nothing about, the pain of a cancer sufferer, the suffering of an abused child or a person who's lost someone dear to them. So, for example, what about the death of a loved one you may ask? That depends on your view of death - of what death is. To many people it's something to be feared, to others it means we go to a 'better' place. There are conditioned responses to death depending on our culture, and beliefs - how we endure the pain of the death of someone close to us depends upon that conditioning. Life however, will always go on and for me, as long as we're alive it's our responsibility to make the best of what's in front of us, even if that's pain - and yes, I've endured a lot of it. We never lose anyone at all, we do however, wish we could've held onto a relationship we've lost and *this* wish is for our own benefit, not the benefit of the person who 'died'. I could give endless examples like this, but these pains - that humanity must currently endure - are caused by the division of humanity from itself; they're the symptoms of a greater illness - the illness of the divided collective mind, currently in destructive 'I' 'Me' 'My' mode. If we were psychologically mature we'd realise that there's much more to us than our bodies and therefore, though we'd feel sorrow if someone close to us died, we'd be far better equipped to cope with it - and to put it into perspective, by knowing that the death of our body is as natural as the birth of it.

~~~

It's often said that we have to do the right things for the right reasons and I'd posture that the same applies to endurance. What do I mean by this? An extreme example might be holding onto a hot iron bar and enduring the pain for no reason other than pride (a challenge perhaps) as opposed to holding onto an iron bar - that has become hot - to keep a door open so
~~~

that people can escape from a burning building. One of these actions is foolish and the other an unselfish act performed in order to save lives. It's not that we've *endured* that's important, but the dignity with which we did it and the strength gained from our experience. The 'condition' of the trail of memories and choices that we leave behind us matters; for example, we can remember a tough childhood as an experience that made us who we are today and in that way positively benefit from it, or we can remember our suffering in a way that perpetuates and accentuates it, preventing us from moving on as we continue to endure the same suffering, re-living it again and again in our minds - I did this for a great many years. There's enough pain and suffering in this world, without us volunteering to unnecessarily endure more. Through dispassionate self-observation we can learn much from the experiences that brought us to where we are at this very moment, and we can share that learning with others, as I'm doing with you. How we approach suffering and how we choose to endure it from this moment on is entirely up to us.

What a
beautiful world.

Life's not
fair.

Plan B

*When we realise the futility of living the
way we do, the process of change has begun.*

If we're honest, the majority of us tend to think of ourselves as inadequate in some way, mostly because we're conditioned to live up to the unattainable standards pushed onto us by society and in particular, by the media. It's inevitable that we'll 'fail' to live up to these standards no matter how hard we try to meet them, because the frontiers keep moving; there's a line that's near on impossible to cross; the competition is fierce and most of us are too tired to fight our way through it. Too many 'hopefuls' are grappling for the same targets; such as, security, romance, beauty, fame, approval or just an ounce of recognition, but the majority of us soon discover that we're 'excess to requirements'; yet *still* we come in droves - ever hopeful and ill-prepared for what lies ahead. We live in a dysfunctional society - one that still has wars, poverty, mass chaos and a burgeoning population - a world full of lies, corruption, external dreams and internal illusions; the world's committing suicide and doesn't give two hoots as long as it's 'business as usual' today - Now Syndrome*. As individuals we're encouraged to do the best we can with our lives - to succeed - but society, as a whole, is more than a little bent on 'failing' - it doesn't do or want what's good for it, but craves what's expedient. 'Plan A' isn't in our best interest and, as avoidable disaster looms, too few people are prepared to give any attention to the possibility of a 'Plan B' - if only we'd give this a little thought.

We divert ourselves from the agonies and frustrations society puts upon us - putting them to the back of our minds; by for example, flexing our muscles at the gym, taking up hobbies, socialising or seeking a good education, but what's the point of any of these; what use are they with regard to the psychological advancement of humanity and what do they really do for us as individuals? These activities do no more than make us look like a better product than we actually are - great packaging on not-so-desirable contents; however, this packaging was designed by those who profit from keeping us in a state of struggle and an illusion that we can be anything other than who we are. We need to be willing to stretch our minds rather than our muscles. The more we try 'to be' something or someone else, the more we thicken our masks and disguises and the less able we are to silence the noise in our minds; we can't see the beauty or simplicity of what lies beneath these masks and therefore, can never reach our full potential. Without peace of mind - whatever we do and wherever we go - we'll face the same problems because that's the world we've elected to live in - a refusal to change what we're doing, is an endorsement to keep things the way they are.

We live by Plan A - what we're doing right now and have been doing all of our lives with no positive change in sight - on the contrary, things in the world are becoming more and more insane and recent elections show that clearly. What I see is choice without choice; a choice between candidates who - according to propaganda - are no better than each other or anyone else for that matter. Despite being fully aware of the hullabaloo, we go along with the drama and *still* choose one of the candidates, whilst complaining about the stupidity of it all, as though we were unable to do anything about the situation. Society expects everyone to vote - to do their 'duty' - so we tend to vote for a candidate who purports to suit our agenda, even though we *know* it's all a contrivance. There's *always* a Plan B - a plan we must elect to implement ourselves and each one of us has the power to choose it, but first we must stop pleading helplessness. Say for example, you're given the choice between eating a rich chocolate fudge cake or an equally rich heavily-iced fruit cake - the debate begins, but as we consider the merits of each offering, we rarely consider the third choice of not eating either one of them, because conditioning demands a choice be made. The choice of not eating isn't *actually* a choice, but rather it's a developed freedom of the mind that doesn't consider either cake - there's no attraction to them. When there's *no* attraction there *is* no decision or consideration necessary; it's something we *feel* rather than have to think about and this feeling puts distance between ourselves and the question - we become mere observers of it.

Most of us have tried to avoid the call of the confectionery aisle in supermarkets at some point in our lives, but then leave the store with a bar of chocolate or packet of something that in some way we regret buying, particularly after we've eaten it. We didn't implement or think about Plan B; however, when we do implement Plan B and manage to leave a supermarket without those 'goodies' we feel pretty good, albeit temporarily as because of our success, we usually reward ourselves on our next scheduled visit, if not sooner. The feel good factor that we experience, in our current state of mind, is so unfamiliar that it gets rejected out of hand because we feel 'unworthy' of sustaining it, causing us to give up almost immediately as our targets are so far away in the future - a future that we may never reach and are willing to trade in for our more immediate desires (Plan A). Have you ever felt on a 'high' after reading a self-help book, going to an aerobics class or perhaps watching an uplifting film? I have. After reading a book many years ago I felt as though I were walking on air. This feeling lasted for about a week, but what I felt was the energy of the book, rather than any of my own, which is why this feeling didn't last any longer. The vast majority of us have experienced this feeling in one form or another *and* the fall that ensues once we settle back into our more familiar mind dramas, problems and routines - our new-found resolve falling by the wayside.

The continuity of the 'lift' we feel living by Plan B happens because we've decided to give our lives a meaning - a meaning that doesn't depend on remuneration or approval and a meaning that enables us to stop doing the things that bring stress, worry and fear into our lives. Take for example, when we look to get fit or to lose a few pounds, deep down we're looking for the approval of others, but mostly for our own; our heart isn't really into the weight loss, but more the image we'll have of ourselves should we succeed. Because we're trying to change our shape we begin with a negative image of ourselves and struggle with various diets, classes and exercise regimes - with varying levels of success. Because we're 'on a diet' we look to when we can come 'off' it, at which point the reverse begins to happen and the process restarts with all the stress and hassle that goes with it. What we really need is a sea change of the way we live and then we'll become healthier and happier with ourselves. More beneficial however, is the sea change for our mind - to filter out the excess daily nonsense that's being fed into it, to remove ourselves from negative situations and to clear out the historical ghosts that haunt us day and night. If we really want our lives to change - we have to *make* those changes, and make them permanent. Plan B requires mental housekeeping and the development of our observational skills - a mastery over ourselves and all that occurs in our lives; it takes time to develop these skills. Though I know this without a shadow of a doubt, I'm still having to work at it.

~~~

Imagine a world where we work and live for the good of each other; a world where humanity gives back as much as it takes and doesn't live in fear of governments or next door neighbours; a world where we care for each other without hatred or hierarchy, without poverty or greed, without fears or locks and without hunger or excess. It's rather hard to do because we're so set in our ways that such a Utopia is nothing more than a distant fantasy, like any other, that can't be fully imagined or realised with our minds in their current state of consciousness - unable to conceive of anything outside it - just as when our curtains are closed we can't see what's on the other side of them. When we begin to see the futility of Plan A, it's like seeing light coming through the cracks of the curtains, which we then draw back enabling ourselves to see the limitless possibilities that lie before us - possibilities that exist beyond the realms of understanding by our Plan A conditioned minds. Plan B!

Plan A is that which is offered to us by society - a plan we delight in complaining about, yet happily follow as it demands nothing of us other than our compliance. Plan B, on the other hand, is facing up to the reality and the futility of Plan A, putting aside our fears of being
~~~

unable to survive without it. Living by Plan B is not a choice *per se*, but more of a realisation that living by Plan A creates havoc in the world. The corollary is that though we no longer need to fully participate in Plan A, we still have to live in the world; therefore, we can't reject the ground we walk on, but rather must strive to leave less of an imprint on it, and for it not to leave its imprint on us. Of course, there's always the danger of trying to fix Plan A with parts of Plan B - to have the best of both worlds - but this won't work because the mindset of Plan B is totally different to that of Plan A; it would be like adding fresh apples to a bowl of rotting ones in the hope of stopping the rot. When we switch to Plan B we arrive at an indefinable space where we're no longer following *any* plan - we instinctively know what we now need to do for the good of humanity *and do it*, even if that contribution might only be a small one, it *is* better than nothing at all. But why are so few people interested in Plan B? Could it be that Plan B demands something of us - a shift from our familiar existence and to do something different? Though many people love to hear or talk about Plan B it's nothing more to them than a flight of fantasy or a 'What if?', never realising that they have the power to make the change today, preferring to dismiss it as a 'not in my life time' phenomenon. Plan B has to be realised for oneself and when it is, what happens next is entirely up to you.

** A term I used in my chapter 'Sensation, Desire and Relevant Reflections'*

A Little More Taking Stock

To climb out of the deep dark hole we dug for ourselves is the hardest thing to do - the key to achieving it is wanting to do it badly enough.

We were born into a living nightmare - no sane person can deny that. As children we struggled to fathom what we saw, looking at it with bewilderment rather than wonder. Even as adults, we've all stood back and looked at the world, knowing that it's crazy as it seamlessly relates to us one frightening story after another - many happening simultaneously; physically, we can't go anywhere else so we do our best to slot in wherever we can - we have to like it or lump it - it's all we've got. An adage I heard a lot in my youth was 'if you can't beat them, join them' - with society the way it is, this isn't exactly good advice'; however, after years of struggling to make sense of a world that *can't* be made sense of, as adults, this is what we tend to do. Such capitulation locks us into a madness that we're both surrounded by and at the mercy of - we become participants at a grotesque masked ball, either dancing or 'sitting one out'. Like guests at the ball, we think we won't be recognised; the majority of us however, can see clearly what lies beneath the masks of others - as clearly as they can see behind ours; they've learnt to fit in just as we have. This knowledge is treated as 'taboo' - a tacit agreement to keep each other's secret while we play out our roles. Without this agreement we'd be stripped of our faux identities and such exposure could cause chaos and confusion; initially, it can be a shock to suddenly be in a position where we judge ourselves, as we've previously judged others.

So we adapt and learn to lie - to fit in with the *status quo*. These lies protect us from ourselves *and* others; we need them in order to hide our underlying vulnerability and because we tell so many of them, they eventually become our truth - the mind supplying the evidence and encouragement we need to convince ourselves of their veracity. I was witness to a good example of this at the time of the 9/11 incident; what happened regarding the actual event is not of concern here, as the mass of information spawning from the incident is so overwhelming that no-one will ever discover what really happened - some know, some think they do and many neither know nor care. Anyway, I mentioned to a friend that I'd seen a video apparently showing a *live* news broadcast from the scene reporting on a building that had collapsed, while it was shown as *still* erect in the background behind the reporter.

Whether or not this film had been manipulated is of no concern to me, but my friend's reaction to this information was that the film studios were *very* busy and probably got their films mixed up - the validity of the information and the integrity of the television company were in her view incontrovertible - she believed that which made her the most comfortable and the idea that the building was simultaneously erect *and* down was 'explained' away, rather than questioned. There's a strange paradox at work in the world whereby 'tongue-in-cheek' we say it must be true as it was 'in the papers' or 'on the television'; however, at the same time, we receive it as a truth; our minds pass it through the filters that present us with a story we can more readily accept - making incidental the parts that don't fit our truth. Perhaps this is why we can so easily watch horror on our screens or read it in our books and newspapers and not cry out loud - we're de-sensitised to it and a horror story on the news has no more inner effect on us than a horror film we watch for pleasure; we don't shed the tears we ought to be drowning in, and would be if we were willing to change our perspective.

It's in our nature to filter out what we don't want to see or hear and turn it into a truth that suits us better. We're unreliable narrators, which is why two people can witness the same incident and - at a later date - give an account of two very different stories about what happened. In much the same way, two people can read the same book or watch the same film and take away different meanings from them; for example, a philosopher and a scientist will dissect the bible in different ways - each finding what they want to find. We might get confused about dates, names, places or faces, but when we tell our stories - particularly if we repeat them often enough - we'll believe them to be true; we all know that this situation causes conflict, particularly in personal relationships. This knowledge opens up all sorts of queries when it comes to thinking about juries or witness statements, and is just one reason why more than one account or opinion is required - even then they can't be relied on. We'll never be capable of judging each other in a way free from all bias, until we've judged ourselves. The mind of humanity is sick, it's confused and doesn't know truth from lies; it doesn't know because it's so caught up in 'I' 'Me' 'My' mode that it can't stand back and observe the bigger picture - also because we have too much irrelevant information in our minds and no room for anything new. If we stood back and took a good look at ourselves - first as individuals and then as a whole - we *would* drown in our own tears. It's then, when we observe ourselves, that the extent of our sickness is revealed. Few of us are prepared to admit to the folly of our own ways - we're not very good at admitting when we're wrong or that we've been foolish; vulnerability in society is strongly discouraged.

To remain in the madness of the world, taking whatever happens to be on offer - whether appealing or not - simply because it's 'sold' to us as a necessity, keeps us coming back for more as we increasingly need to alleviate the mental and physical pains of living, which paradoxically, are caused by the very quest to alleviate them - making it all hurt so much more. We make the most of what's available, enjoying the entertainment, material things and other distractions while we have the opportunity to do so, but this is a grab-it-while-you-can attitude towards life that throws caution to the wind, regardless of the consequences for ourselves or future generations - it's been done this way for a long time. We don't consider what we're *actually* doing, why we're living in a nightmare we can't seem to wake from, or why we're unable to live freely without the need for outside authority. We allow our minds to be manipulated and they've become twisted and dulled beyond recognition. We gave up asking the innocent questions of our childhood because they were frowned upon and considered to be 'childish'; as a result, we slowly developed a thoughtless and carefree attitude towards life, desiring only the pleasures we could find in it - our hearts hardened.

~~~

It occurred to me while writing this chapter that I've never really thought about what an adult is. I know that it's a 'big person' and that it somewhat eagerly, assumes control of its life when it 'comes of age'. I know also that adults pay more for tickets and can get into places and do things that are for 'adults only', but what actually *is* an adult? Our influences and beliefs change gradually over the course of our lifetimes - so gradually that we don't notice them - but after a while the metamorphosis from innocent child into adult is blatant. There are many ways to describe what an adult is, but mostly it's an innocent child who as a result of successful indoctrination and growing 'bigger' can now do the things that were on their banned list when they were small, without the risk of censure or having to provide identification to prove that they're of 'legal age'; for example, to buy alcohol, tobacco or x-rated materials. In other words, 'adult' is a license to do all the things forbidden to the innocent - most often carried out behind closed doors. An adult has learnt to abide by the rules of an unwell society and to enforce those same rules upon 'newcomers' to the human race - towering over them as indoctrinators and thus carrying on the cycle. Adults are under the
~~~

illusion that they're in control of their world, whereas they're actually *out* of control. Amongst other things, being an adult is also a licence to behave badly - very badly if we choose to do so. I suppose in some ways, you could compare the psychological process of becoming an adult to an expanding balloon (creating our egos); society blows information into the balloon and as it does the balloon inflates; the process of unlearning can be likened to deflating the balloon - returning to a state of innocence - which is *not* the same as being 'childish' or 'naïve'.

When we were young and innocent we believed everything we were told, not because we were naïve or stupid, but rather because we loved and trusted the people we were surrounded and directed by - our care was entirely in their hands. We loved the stories they told and were protected from the 'news' and other adult occupations as we were generally - in my day at least - tucked up in bed at these times. Slowly, as we grew older, the levels of corruption and frustration of our world dawned on us; such as, the world is a tough place to live in, it's not fair, Father Christmas isn't all he seems to be and neither are our myths or legends - we felt let down, ill-prepared for life and very much alone. For all the knowledge we've been given we still have no idea what we're doing or who we are. In many ways we're worse off than the innocent children we once were - at least then we had something or someone we could put our trust in - something to believe in, or hope for. But not all is lost. By returning to our innocence we combine the best of being a child with that of an adult and come to realise that the only person we can really put our trust in is ourselves - our lives are now in our own hands, with all that implies. Reflecting on this helps us develop an understanding of our circumstances, but not the knowledge of how we found ourselves so vulnerable in them - what lies before and beyond our lives must, it seems, remain a mystery for now. When we answer our 'call', our attention turns away from the horror and sorrow of this world - which we can't change - back to a state of wonderment at our surroundings, but this time in awe of them rather than bewilderment.

Stepping out of Time

*When we step out of time we also step out of space
and can find ourselves somewhat out of tune.*

We can march in time, keep in step with this world and all it has to offer, good or bad, accepting the *status quo* and our eventual demise, or we can dare to step out of time, aspire to greater heights and march to our own rhythm.

As far as we can tell - due to our limited perspective - the reality in which we live is finite; there's a beginning and an end - the part in the middle is what we call life. Like it or not, we're governed by laws we didn't vote for - the laws of the physical universe, from whichever scientific discipline, that control every aspect of our lives. We take many of them for granted; when we lay a table for a meal we expect the plates and cutlery to stay where we put them - not to float off somewhere less convenient; those same laws cause our vases to break if we drop them. Scientists have tried to understand these physical laws and use them to our advantage - or disadvantage - by combining them *or* using one against the other; for example, getting a plane to lift off the ground or finding new ways to devastate entire cities. With such focus on the physical side of our world it's hardly surprising there's no place for the extraordinary - thinking is 'well-grounded' and 'conclusive'; there's nothing that can't be explained away by good scientific reasoning. Should anything extraordinary raise its head, there are any number of well-meaning (or not as the case may be) learned journals, professors, teachers or rationalists down the pub to explain the phenomenon away to their own satisfaction, based on their biases and experiences. There's no room for miracles in this physical materialistic world and the entertaining of such is considered the forte of religious crack-pots or those needing to see a psychiatrist, so that they can be re-integrated into the 'real world'. There's a reluctance to consider stepping out of this physical existence, to contemplate the metaphysical or to go beyond what we *think* we know - it's out of our comfort zone. We brush aside our non-physical nature - which is as much a part of us as our hands and feet are - preferring, it seems, the mind-numbing 'around the clock' familiarity of the existence that keeps us firmly entrenched in the physical mind-set, until our inevitable demise.

~~~

I made it down a long flight of stairs by taking just two steps; I've done the same thing before without taking any steps at all and sometimes I don't make it to the bottom of the stairs as they morph into a path through a forest, or I find myself walking along a beautiful sandy seashore ... I'm driving a car but the road ahead of me disappears and then I'm surrounded by walls that are shrinking the space around me, but I don't crash into them and they soon morph into something else and in a flash I'm walking our dog in the countryside or sitting
~~~

at my desk, which may or may not be in my home - where it should be. I cross a road in a single step and as I put my foot down the path I thought I'd stepped onto dissolves into a giant puddle and I watch, fascinated, as the ripples spread out. I walk on water and walk through walls; sometimes I even fly and once I had a houseful of friends all speaking in what I thought was Chinese - I understood them - though I can't speak a word of it.

No, I haven't lost the plot; I'm talking about dreams. Dreams are strange because they don't make sense and defy what we think of as the laws of physics - the laws that trap us in what we know as 'reality'. Strangely, in our dreams, nothing seems to be out-of-place or give rise to concern - it all seems perfectly 'normal'. When we wake from these dreams, we can no longer do the impossible and find ourselves once again limited by the restrictions of time and space. There are enough books and opinions on what dreams, out-of-body experiences and illusions are and, as always, science is doing its best to explain these things to us - saving us the trouble of thinking for ourselves. However, I like to explore my world for myself and observe what I see, which if you think about it is what the authors of books, purveyors of opinions and scientists do as well - so I'm going to talk about how these things occur in *my* world, because this *is* my world and *everything* in it is coming from my mind - how can it possibly come from anywhere else.

On the point of defying the 'laws of physics' in our dreams; so what? Dreams are as much a part of our lives as our day-to-day activities are when we're awake. The laws of physics are concerned with matter and energy, yet so much about us is non-physical; for example, our minds, dreams and imaginations; why do we need sleep, or why do we dream. Much of our life is spent asleep and somehow we don't consider the relevance of this. We see sleeping as essential rest from the day's activities that exhaust us - sometimes collapsing into a heap on our beds, until the following morning when we start those activities all over again, perhaps beginning our first conversation of the day with 'I had this really weird dream last night' and after recounting it, never giving it another thought. There's more to our sleep than that. We drift into unconsciousness, as day drifts into night; there's no proof whatsoever that we're anywhere at all when we're asleep, even if there's a witness who states that they saw us lying in our bed. Does the world exist at all when we're not 'here'? This question is increasingly interesting for me.

As a child and well into my adulthood I experienced repeating dreams; I woke up at the same point each time - other dreams had recurring themes running through them in a variety of different situations. One of these themes is 'voicelessness'. I've often been calling out to someone I wanted to help in some way, or warn against an impending danger, but no sound comes out of my mouth - as though I were mute - and I feel unable to move closer to them. Sometimes there are other people around and I call out for assistance, but still I've no voice. Usually this voicelessness dream occurs when someone is drowning in the sea or sinking into the land or quicksand; I hold my hand out, stretching it as far as I can, but can't reach the hand they're holding out to me.

I used to find this dream disconcerting and frustrating. I'd watch until the person disappeared completely and then wake up in a sweat. So what could these dreams be about? In my younger years I'd often see simple solutions to other people's problems, but was rarely asked for my opinion and to have given it when it wasn't asked for - which I did on numerous occasions - was akin to pulling a dog's tail; I learnt this lesson the hard way. Perhaps the hand in the dream was not really reaching out to me, but to someone else that I couldn't see - or perhaps the person holding out their hand wanted to drag me down with them. No doubt there are many possible interpretations, but the way I see it, we re-write our waking reality in our dreams, removing time and space, making them surreal and adding extra drama. Just as in my dreams, I couldn't help anyone in 'real life' and had no voice - no-one listened. What I've learnt from realising this is that we can't help people who don't want to be helped, even if they appear to be reaching out to us.

It has been said that if we die in a dream we die in 'real life', but I don't see how anyone could possibly prove it. I seemingly died many times in dreams from being shot, falling or being hit by a car. I can't say for sure that I wouldn't have survived these experiences as I subsequently woke up, with the odd feeling that I'd somehow dropped back into my body. I'd suggest that perhaps it's the same with 'near death experiences' for no-one can see beyond death; no-one can see beyond the mystery of life - we can only speculate and speculation comes from conditioned memories. I'd suggest that our dreams are a form of housekeeping - where we can work on unresolved issues and fears - and just as with the clutter in a house that hasn't been touched for years, the contents of our minds are in a state of disarray. We each have one home (our mind) and in it are stored all the moments of our lives - every touch, taste, wish, hope, joy, ache, pain and heartbreak. There's much mind-management to be done before we can see our world more clearly and only we can do that work - no-one else can do it for us. When we make a start on our 'housekeeping' there can be a lot of dust and clutter to work through, but gradually we come to know and realise many things; such as, our five senses lock us into believing this physical world is real and 'all there is' - they confirm its existence and apparent solidity and deny any other explanation or exploration - all of our physical experiences have come through our senses.

When we're prepared to step out of time, our spiritual sense opens up a whole new world of possibilities, but like the sailors of old, who were frightened to sail too close to the horizon in case they fell off the edge of the world, we can experience similar fears of the unknown - we've become so locked into the physical world that we're afraid to step out of it. Magic and spirituality have become 'spooky' themes that are explained away as 'fantasy' by the realm of entertainment and in so doing, come to have no more meaning than amusing hocus pocus - or not so amusing horror (though entertaining for some of us). If we choose to *stay* in time then we'll continue to be haunted by the memories and events of our pasts, and those of others too - such as the victims of war. Our past is *full* of horrors and our future is going to be bleak, if we continue to do what we're doing - causing and perpetuating mischief in our world.

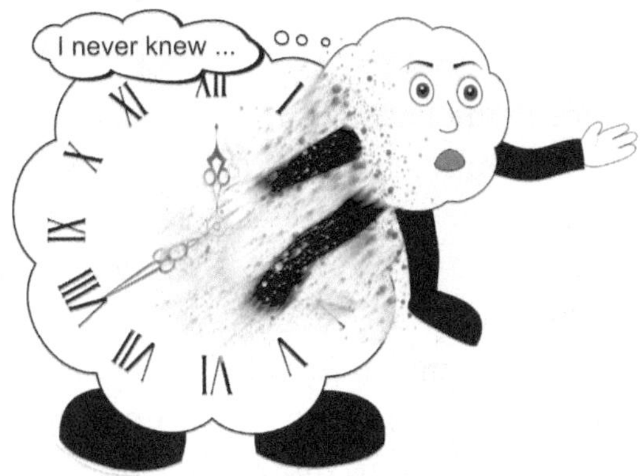

By 'stepping out of time' we connect to something different - something indefinable and unfamiliar - but to connect to this we need to disconnect - mentally - from the way we're living now. We can do this by realising not only the illusory nature of the world we live in but the negligent way in which we live in it - a negligence that's causing our world to go downhill fast - filling it with sorrow, unnecessary illness and destruction along the way. When we open our eyes - perhaps peeping through our fingers - to some painful truths, we gradually become aware of our surroundings in a new way; our world becomes surreal and less scary and the monsters we once closed our eyes to aren't there anymore. However, we have to *stay* connected to this mindset otherwise we'll revert to our old habits, hear the same old song we've always heard, and the monsters will reappear. The very act of stepping out of one situation places us into another, just as though we were walking from one room to the next.

The quality of our experience in this world depends on the choices we make; for example, what film to watch, what career to pursue or which train to take. The memories from whichever film we choose to watch get etched onto our minds and inevitably weave themselves into our dreams; the career we choose will shape many parts of our lives and the next train we board could turn out to be a life or death situation. We hold onto bitterness, anger, vengeance, spite and other unhealthy feelings that come from our past, without realising that they not only destroy our future, but turn our dreams into nightmares - they're internalised and control our lives, harming only ourselves rather than our chosen 'targets'. Our lives are fragile yet we live them carelessly and thoughtlessly assuming that tomorrow will always arrive because it's noted - in so many different ways - on our calendars. We're here to write our own lyrics, play our own music and dance our own dance, but the problem is we're doing it under the clockwork direction of external influence and conditioning; we should be playing in our own 'one man band' - considerately - for the benefit of ourselves and others, but somewhere along the line our lives were hijacked and we're now dancing to someone else's tune.

Time; we live by it, eat by it, work by it, play by it and at an *unknown* time we're going to have to 'die' by it. I mentioned earlier that many seem to prefer the mind-numbing 'around the clock' familiarity of our physical mind-set, but there's so much more to us if we dare to contemplate the metaphysical, and go beyond what we *think* we know. *Now* is the time, our chance, our opportunity to do just that, while the clock is still ticking.

A Touch of Feeling

When we feel love for ourselves,
we'll feel love for all others.

Life is something we have to fully experience to the end; we can't run away from caring about the outside world, and expect to feel happy on the inside.

We *all* have feelings but do we ever intelligently think about what they are? As with all my questions, the more I think about them the more obscure they become, yet all my life I've spoken about my feelings and the feelings of people I've come into contact with. We 'feel' every moment of our lives, even in our dreams, and we'd not get far without doing so - feelings are an essential part of us. As with all subjects that I begin to focus on, the experience is like opening a trunk; the contents of which unpack themselves as we rummage through it. We begin to see things we already know very well and have no need for external references to back up what we find; having said that, discussing the subject with like-minded people can be fun and reveal even more, provided the parties concerned are listening to each other. As I'm making notes, it becomes clear that this is an *enormous* subject that can't be contained in one chapter, let alone a book, so I'm going to skim over what opening up the trunk has revealed to me so far.

What is a feeling? Essentially, it's a sense - our feelings allow us to be sensitive to all that we're surrounded by. We have five senses that confirm our physical world, but we also have senses that relate to the 'metaphysical' and we refer to them frequently without realising it; examples are:

- I feel you're upset about something.
- The experience left a bad taste in my mouth.
- I see what you mean.
- I smell a rat.
- I heard a voice inside my head.
- I feel like I'm being watched.
- I sense danger.
- I was touched by their generosity.

A feeling is a body, egoic or other metaphysical reaction relating to an event - external or internal; such as another person, a passion, a suspicion or for that matter, anything we come into contact with or have experienced - it begins with thought. By bodily reaction I mean, for example, when we come out in goose-bumps or break out in a cold sweat - by egoic reaction, when we take offense or have our pride hurt. Like the physical five senses, our feelings and emotions make us aware of the external world. Through these feelings we experience fear, sadness, happiness, danger and many other reactions that we express as emotions - we couldn't exist without them. Whereas our metaphysical senses allow us to be *aware* of our world, our five physical senses confirm its *existence* and help us to navigate our way through it. Without these senses we can't experience the world, though we *can* manage with the loss of some of them as is the case with those of us who are unable to hear, speak or see. The majority of us - including me - can't imagine what it would be like to live in a world where we can't see, touch, taste, hear or smell. We need at *least* one of our physical senses to confirm that we're living in a world *at all* and therein lies a good philosophical argument for existence itself - an argument that can't be tested because it can never be completely experienced.

Let's expand on an item from the above list - 'I *feel* like I'm being watched'. Remember, that this is *only* a feeling with no physical evidence to back it up - we've no idea where it came from or why we're feeling it, but it can have a great effect on us. Our minds '*real-ise*' the experience and won't leave it alone - *physicalising* and emotionalising it. The feeling of being watched leaves us with uncomfortable emotions of uncertainty, insecurity or vulnerability as our personal space appears to have been invaded from afar. These emotions can pass through us in a flash or linger and compound, depending on the attention we're prepared to give them - possibly leading to further upset, tears or even blind panic, depending on the situation. If we're outdoors at the time of this feeling we usually look around to ensure our security and, if we're indoors and discover - or believe - that we really *are* being watched we may decide to close the curtains and check that our doors and windows are locked. In both cases, our reaction - physical and emotional - tends to come from a place of fear rather than certainty. Our reaction to the feeling of 'being watched' (true or imagined) is based on what our minds have absorbed - much of it horror and other negativity - and our imagination, feeding on these memories, creates a fearful experience.

To digress a little, I'd suggest that the root of the 'feeling of being watched' began when we were babies; we've *always* been watched and continue to be watched - also criticised or compared - in one way or another by our parents, siblings, teachers, friends, employers and surveillance equipment. We've become so accustomed to being watched that we not only *feel* it, but now also watch ourselves *and* each other - walking along the street, in mirrors, through windows or keyholes, at work, at play and on social media etc. The result of continuous observation and comparison - leading to our inevitable self-micro-management - is what causes us to become self-conscious; we've been moulded, criticised, cajoled or even abused into a 'shape' that a fractured and disgruntled society finds acceptable. This distorted image of ourselves becomes, not what we *are* but what we've come to *believe* we are - an image we go all out to protect in order to *remain* acceptable - so that we still exist - and this is what makes us emotionally fragile - we become defensive. Our intense conditioning prevents us from thinking about ourselves as we *truly* are, because we've become so attached to the images of 'I' 'Me' and 'My'. We don't have the ability to fully conceive the truth about ourselves and no-one can convince us otherwise until we want to see it - we wouldn't believe them. However, we *do* have 'feelings' that tell us quite clearly that there's more to us than our wardrobes, tax numbers or social media profiles; we're frauds - we know it - we *feel* it.

~~~

Feelings we can't contain, or control, plague our minds day and night - they cause us to lose sleep and wake the following morning often more tired than when we went to bed. Sometimes this is in excited anticipation of an event such as Christmas day, starting a new job, going on holiday, our last day at school or perhaps our birthday, but at other times the 'plague' follows an event, like being left standing at the aisle, the death of a family member or a heated argument we got into; in these situations our feelings are so intense that we can't be cheered up or reasoned with. I'm sure many of us have tossed and turned all night - over a situation we could've handled differently - re-playing the scene as it actually happened including feeling all the emotions we felt at the time *and* - with the benefit of hindsight - re-writing our various preferred versions of it. In the case of a death in the family, or a friend for that matter, the emotions of 'regret' and 'remorse' torture us about things we failed to do; such as, 'I could've been kinder', 'I shouldn't have said this or that', 'I never said *I love you*', 'I shouldn't have wished you harm' or 'I put off saying sorry for too long' - all of which are now too late to remedy; we tend to take time for granted - thinking we've plenty of it - and then beat ourselves up when it runs out.

Our mind dramas come from events in our pasts or anticipated futures, but the emotions we feel are always in the Now. If we focus on this fact as and when the
~~~

dramas take place we gain a greater awareness of how our minds work; watching our thoughts and reactions to whatever life puts in front of us, as and when it happens - life becomes a 'Live' event rather than a review of the past. With this realisation comes the ability to free ourselves from the restraints of our pasts - regardless of whether events took place fifteen years or fifteen minutes ago - nothing good can come from dwelling on them. It can take a while to adapt our way of thinking, but I promise that if you persevere and repeat the exercise it'll become clear. Old habits can take a long time to free ourselves from; they're past events we *prefer* to repeat and hold onto rather than evict - they literally 'in-habit' us. We'll still feel sorrow and pain when things go wrong in our lives or don't go the way we want them to - it's a part of our human condition, but we'll be better equipped to heal ourselves and put things into perspective, instead of allowing our feelings to get in the way of intelligent judgement and action - it takes practise.

Life isn't fair - it never has been. I was placed into an orphanage at the age of nine months and had to live with all the dramas that go with such a predicament. At the time I was too young to control events in my life, or society's will to crush me - a task I later took over responsibility for. To my knowledge, we've no control on where, when or to whom we're born; however, as we grow older we have the power to make choices that shape our world and the most major of those choices is to take back control of our lives, by not allowing the past or society to intimidate or guide us - we can't change them when we're children, but we *can* remove their strong and erroneous influence once we reach adulthood. If we choose *not* to then the past and present situation in society will continue to control how we think, feel and behave for the best part of our lives - feeling all the unwanted emotions that go with that decision.

~~~

There are times when our emotions are remembered - like a gun that fires a bullet when the trigger is pulled or a light that comes on when the switch is flicked; we carry these dormant emotions around with us for our whole lives and they can be highly destructive. Remembered emotions lie dormant until an external action is applied, like a wrong word someone says to us, a large utility bill that arrives in the post or the sight of a long forgotten enemy - perhaps from our school days. In the case of the first example we may associate the word with an unpleasant past event and it can feel like re-living an experience we've no wish to re-live - in the second case we may feel the emotion of frustration at once again being short of funds. The third example is more complicated as an enemy from our school days would probably invoke *many* nasty emotions that we've no wish to return to feeling and, believed we'd left behind us. Another example of a remembered emotion is that which we long to feel again, because to be without the feeling is too painful; for example, when we 'fall in love' because we *need* to be in love or when we're on the rebound - neither of which are in our best interest.

We need to learn how to re-act to situations that recur in our lives by recognising that we lash out to
~~~

protect ourselves from re-experiencing things that disturbed us in the past. If we don't learn this, then we'll spend the rest of our lives feeling angry, defensive, snappy, sulky, uncertain of ourselves or seeking to re-experience happy 'times gone by' - taking us away from the life that's happening *now* - *not* in the past. We don't necessarily know that we're remembering an emotion when we react to triggers; too often these emotions are buried deep within us and because they're unresolved, exert a force that manifests itself as over-sensitivity - an adult can display out of proportion reactions to even the smallest slight if he was subjected to hyper-criticism as a child.

~~~

Up until now I've discussed our *own* feelings, but it's important to widen our perspective and examine how we actually feel about others when, for example, we pass a crash scene - most of us would be horrified to realise how limited our feelings are for the people involved. Almost everyone in the world is in pain and has suffered as much, perhaps more, than we have. We like our social media pages to be filled with 'inspirational' material, but we blend this inspiration with horror on our next post - not unlike 'have longer eye lashes' advertisements between earthquake or other disaster news flashes. How can we change this situation? One of the best ways to do this is to recognise that our emotions are erratic and irrational - we change from one moment to the next, forgetting - or not recognising - what matters most. We like to think that we're caring, loving and warm people;
~~~

that may be the case amongst our close-knit family and friends but how many of us extend that warmth to those who don't live in our relatively small social circles - those we tend to pass by or comfort with charitable pennies or empty words - some of us don't even spare those. Think about beggars, an elderly person we brush past, a passed-out drunkard or the homeless in the street for example; we can be unkind in our judgements of these people - judgements we've been conditioned to feel; these people are not only symptoms of the dysfunctional and selfish environment that we've created, they serve as unwelcome reminders of it.

When we meet another person we don't tend to see their pain as we're more focused on what they look like, what they do for a living, how scruffily they're dressed, who does their hair or perhaps what they can do for us

- socialising etc. But inside each beggar, elderly person, passed-out drunkard or homeless person whose path we cross is a sad story that has left them in their unfortunate circumstances; their world is very lonely and generally, we feel no real compassion or pity for them - we don't even acknowledge them.

When did we stop caring outside of our personal circle? To share in the sadness of another person is a difficult thing, especially when we're generally unable to help them out of their situation other than to offer a few words of comfort or hold their hand. Our ability to sympathise is largely limited to feeling apologetic for someone's situation - and to commiserate with them, but we can't really help them beyond that; their pain persists until they reach a point where they're able to lessen it or let it go - which is sometimes never. We see worldwide pain and suffering every day of our lives through our various media outlets - some of it horrifying and all of it unacceptable. We *have* to look away and forget about it, as most of the stories are so far away from where we live and work that we're unable to offer help - other than financial - which history proves is never a solution to the problem - or we can expose the news, by forwarding the stories to others in the hope that *they'll* be able to do something about it. We have our own problems to think about that are closer to home; we've the dog to walk, bills to pay, plumbing to fix, shopping, work to do, kids to feed and we're always on the 'Go' 'Go' 'Go' for one reason or another - such are the lifestyles we've unwisely created - *we're* in pain too..

Back to the question from another perspective 'When did we stop caring … ?' I don't believe we ever did - we maxed-out on empathy. We've empathised with so many situations that we're now exhausted, with nothing left to give to the sick, poor, tragic or hopeless - there are too many of them. The suffering of others has become the 'norm' and we no longer *see* the beggars in the street *or* realise that we walk around them as though they were a fixture, like a bollard. Whatever we *personally* do, it'll never be enough to stop the flow of suffering - we can't see the end of it. Stories in the news have become no more than our daily 'infotainment' - topics of 'cultured' or 'educated' discussion to spread, 'like' or 'thumbs up' on our media pages - they're no longer remarkable. So we shop, work, stop at coffee shops, entertain, amuse and occupy ourselves so that we don't have to think about or feel the outside world, but however much we do those things it still exists. The outside world is as much a part of us as our inside world but we feel powerless to change the first and unable to change the second; we *can* make choices in our personal 'circles' that make a difference to our lives (to have a baby or not, for example) - regardless of whether it's a positive or negative difference; the point is, it's something we have control over and we *like* to feel that we're in control.

Due to our conditioning, whether we like to believe we're conditioned or not, we don't fully understand our feelings or emotions - we don't talk easily about them. In many cases, feelings and emotions are things we've learnt to hide because it's 'sissy' or 'weak-minded' to show them; we're taught that we should be strong and able to take the blows of life without complaining about them. We're 'case-hardened' - or think we are - and expect others to be too. Because of this we're not always in control of our feelings as much as we'd like to be; for example, giving full rein to emotions like anger, rage, aggression, jealousy, extended sorrow or sadness. These emotions - uncontrolled - are damaging not only to ourselves, but also to those on the receiving end of them. That we have these emotions is part of our human experience, but learning to keep them under control is an art we're far from mastering. We've all felt anger welling up inside us and to a large extent it's because we allowed its seed to sprout and our egos to water it, until it could no longer be contained. By observing how we react to various situations that we regularly and *repeatedly* encounter, we get to know that our emotions are out of control. When we *do* take an honest look at ourselves, and especially at how we react to others - watching the 'Live Event' - we begin to understand our feelings and emotions - we become emotionally mature. Such maturity makes us better equipped to deal with situations that arise - we begin to sympathise and empathise with others, rather than criticising or lashing out at them.

It's said that empathy is 'head' and sympathy 'heart'. Where that originates I've no idea and in my opinion it's irrelevant as are the origins of pity or compassion. We spend too much time analysing, labelling and mapping these things and not enough time *intelligently* feeling them. I say what does it matter where they come from as long as we're able to feel for and help other people - as long as we can say 'No, it's not okay that our world is like this' and *mean* it. Yes, empathy and sympathy are different, but they don't come from different places; I'd suggest that they come from our minds (which can't be located) - from the thoughts that are our experiences and in particular from our conditioned thoughts and responses. Feeling empathy and sympathy represent 'kindness' and *this* is what the world needs to focus on - not single trendy 'acts' of kindness; such as 'Free Hugs Here', but *ongoing* kindness towards everyone - a kindness mindset. When we turn our attention away from ourselves, it automatically turns towards the rest of the world; then - and only then - can we feel the pain, hear the voice and look into the eyes of others - only then can we empathise with the rest of humanity and be able to see the beggar, instead of the bollard.

Gratitude

*Gratitude is the appreciation of things
not deserved, earned or demanded.*

When we look inside *ourselves* we find a different world - a world much larger than the one we're familiar with and a world that's so full of revelations, that had someone recounted this knowledge to us, we wouldn't have believed them. For example, we discover how focused we are in 'I' 'Me' 'My' mode and don't give much thought to the rest of the world, as long as we're okay - our new world reveals much that we don't tend to like admitting about ourselves. Paradoxically, this process changes all we see on the outside too - it *must*, in the same way as changing our appearance changes what we see in a mirror. The world becomes a mystery again - a mystery that's been waiting for us to delve into it. We can unravel this mystery as far as it'll allow us to and in doing so, it reveals those beautiful things we've taken for granted for so long. Again, paradoxically, the more we unravel the mystery the more of a mystery it becomes; however, something's different, *something* we're unable to put into words, *something* that changes our outlook on life bringing with it an energy that inspires and motivates us to explore further, and *something* that we can't show or adequately explain to another person.

On our journey, what we need to discover more than anything else are our *own* eyes, and we find them when we begin to piece together the puzzle of life - a puzzle that can't be explained until we come upon it for ourselves. Up until now we've tended to look at the world in a way that's expected of us; for example, being grateful that things aren't much worse than they are, being grateful that we *have* a job, being grateful that there's no war in *our* country and being grateful for our possessions. These are the things we're told we should be grateful for - we're 'guilted' into feeling bad about having something that's an inalienable right, by images and stories of people who have less than we do. As a child, when I didn't like something on my dinner plate, I was told I should be grateful for it and continually reminded about how many children around the world weren't as fortunate as I was - we grow up with a sense of guilt. Every one of us has a right to live in peace and to have enough food, water and shelter. Our encouragement to be grateful for these 'essential for living' things is a diversion - it keeps us from seeing the things we really *should* feel gratitude for; it also encourages us to be grateful for things that are 'sold' back to us - like water - but they're already ours. We *share* this planet and no one person has more right to the water on it than another. This sort of encouraged gratitude is not gratitude at all, but rather it instils the fear that we may one day not have water, food or shelter - a fear not lost on a society that encourages dependence on it to provide for our needs. Consequently, we comply with a system that demands we adequately prepare for our old age - which we may never reach - instead of living now, and also that we live in fear of going hungry, thirsty or living on the streets. One side effect of this fear is that we become self-protective thus, as the years pass, we care first and foremost for ourselves; another effect is that we're far too busy with our day-to-day activities to think about the core of our existence.

~~~

Gratitude isn't a reply to a fulfilled desire or something that's happened to us by chance. I remember once coming home and as I reached the gate having tears running down my face; I wore a huge smile at the same time and had no idea why, but did feel grateful 'to be' in this state of what I can only describe as joy. Gratitude is a thankfulness that passes through us; it's there one minute and gone the next, but it leaves a lasting memory of that moment that we don't forget, though we've no idea why this feeling of gratitude arose in us in the first place. A few years back these happy teary
~~~

moments occurred to me all the time; I'd come back from shopping and enter the house in tears - prompting questions asking me what was wrong, but these moments were beyond explanation - they were to be experienced, not analysed. After a while, my 'moments' were just smiled at and accepted as something that was happening to me - a change taking place. Eventually, the tears and smiles gave way to what I can only describe as a profound understanding - I'd changed. Gratitude is a state of mind that can't be expressed by words or actions - such as 'thank you' or exchanging gifts; as our awareness grows, it develops into a 'state' of appreciation that alters the way we approach life.

I find myself trying to remember when these feelings began and I can't be sure, but I do know that it was at a time when I was prepared to take back 'control' of my life. That is to say, I was no longer living in expectation that good things would come knocking at my door or looking to find any happiness outside of myself, or in anybody else for that matter - I'd stopped feeling hard-done-by and began taking responsibility for my life. I put myself in the driving seat and had no idea where my journey would end; I *still* don't, but I *do* know that my life now has purpose and that I alone am responsible for the choices I make *and* the consequences of those choices. Being in the driving seat means I can observe and react to - or not as the case may be - my actions and thoughts as and when they occur. Through such inner observation - if we're prepared to reflect on what we find - we come to realise that we're judgemental, hypocritical, envious, jealous, critical and spiritually aimless. Probably the most insightful revelations are that we're not the perfect beings we once thought ourselves to be, that we knew this all along and that life isn't a battle between us and the rest of the world, but rather a battle to overcome ourselves - our inimitable egos - and in doing so, we develop a new and wider-angled understanding of the outside world.

The more we know and accept about ourselves, the more we're able to discern - without prejudice - what we see on the outside. Acknowledging our own behaviour and reactions to events that occur in our lives causes a change in us - we 'grow *up*' in our awareness, raising our vibration and reconnecting to a higher knowledge; it's to this phenomenon that I attribute the joyful teary moments I mentioned earlier. However, if we continue to live our lives focusing our attention on the outside without growing 'up', then we'll always be in a state of looking for that *something* 'missing' in our lives, but never finding it. We don't know what that something is, but we'll never feel complete without it and have nothing to feel truly grateful for. Realising this not only 'lightens our load', but brings clarity to our lives in a way that inspires gratitude, enabling us to live serenely, instead of trying to cram everything we can into our lives before our inevitable 'demise' - the pressure is off. The clock still ticks, the world still spins, everyone gets on with their business and it's all happening very nicely without our full attention, as it always did; what changes is our attachment to it - our fears subside, we're less self-engrossed and no longer need approval or approbation. The world reacts to us according to how *we* react to it; everything outside is what we perceive and how we choose to interact with that perception.

The seed of gratitude is planted when our perception of the world changes - when we learn to see it more fully. As long as we see the world as something we have to function in - effectively 'clocking in' when we wake up to become part of the machine and 'clocking out' again when we fall asleep - we'll be unable to see the beauty and mystery of it - a mystery we're not here to solve, but to discover, learn and grow 'up' from during the course of our lives, however long - or short - they may turn out to be. When gratitude grows in us it alters our attitude towards the outside world - our focus of attention changes and with it our priorities; we're no longer attached to the material things that once attracted us, because we see the temporary nature of things - they no longer hold us captive.

We're all challenged in one way or another and those challenges are irrelevant when talking about gratitude. What matters is *how* we live our lives and that we learn to live virtuously at every moment, rather than living in a past that we *allow* to define and therefore limit us. No matter what our circumstances we can all appreciate the beauty of life, the mysteries within it and live with every part of our being - physical and metaphysical - so that we become whole. Our world becomes a larger place (in our mind) in a smaller space, with no need to explore outside for what we'll never find - that innate 'Who am I?' knowledge that we seek. I walk down the street, but no longer feel intrinsically part of it; I'm watching the world from a different space and I'm grateful for that -

grateful to *know* that I'm on a journey - with a purpose - when before I was so lost, needy, insecure, going from one birthday to another, one home to another, one marriage to another, one fashion to another and above all, one mistake to another. I'm done searching for my place in this world because I've found it, inside, and my wish is to help others to find theirs.

If I Told You

Disappointment is anticipation turned to ashes.

When we've had enough. When life feels meaningless. When we can't see where we're going and wonder what we're doing here at all, we've two choices. We can bob up and down in the river of our thoughts (content or otherwise) - which I did for a long time - or we can strike out for the bank and hope there'll be something there when we climb out. Knowledge that there's *something* beyond this existence comes from a continuous investigation of ourselves, a willingness to turn over every stone and most importantly, not to give up when things get tough. Things *do* get tough and we can often wonder what point there is in continuing, but it's only a wave and when we're vigilant, it doesn't take long before we recognise the pattern of those waves coming and going, or to know that we can be carried closer to the bank with each wave we encounter - if we choose not to drown beneath it.

Why should I bother?
You could at least try Dilly.

Turning back is *not* an option.

137

If I told you
That our pains are not worth keeping
That our worries aren't worth weeping
Would you let it all go,
If I told you
That our fears are all unfounded
That our tears are all unsounded
Could you let it all go, if I told you …

Or would you hold on tightly to it
Let it rule and break your spirit
Build a wall and not smash through it,
If I told you
And if I showed you all your might
Would you stand right up and fight
Or meekly crumble to the floor
Forever suffer more and more.

If I told you
What we seek is all inside
That we've never really tried
Would you let it all go,
If I told you
That your feet have not been grounded
That we leave this life astounded
Would you let it all go, if I told you …

Or would you show your frozen heart
Shout and scream and fall apart
Pin a point upon your chart,
If I told you
And if I showed you all your power
Would you climb up to that tower
Or continue on your path
Always cry and never laugh

If I show you
That it's pointless to delay
That the beast is ours to slay
That it's love that we deny
How the mind is cruel and sly
That the pains of yesterday
Are now very far away
That there's no point laying low
That it's life we must outgrow
When we walk around that bend
It's ourselves we must befriend
That our tears need not be cried
Only you and I decide

Would you let it all go, if I told you ...

Wrapping Up

Tears that fall on barren land produce nothing
- they're cried in vain.

Our lives are short; at one extreme, they're so short that we don't even get the chance to blink and at the other they seem to drag on for so long that we want 'out' - particularly if we're frail and in bad health. Few of us take the time to ponder the meaning of our lives and though we're unable to fully determine where we come from, who we are or where we're going, we *are* able to feel an innate 'sense' that there's more to us than this life; for me, this couldn't be more clear, but I've had to start from scratch by questioning *everything* I've ever been taught, without taking in more rogue information. In the past we were educated to search for information in museums, libraries, books or to listen to our teachers; nowadays, we turn to the internet as the font of all wisdom, but it's only humanity's 'recycle bin'. This is fine if we want to know how to bake a cake or determine the molecular weight of lead, but not much use in our search to find out who we are. The internet is far from being wise, but it *is* bursting with everything we've explored, hidden and revealed or don't want to know about; none of the information can be relied on when asking the question 'Who am I?' All we can expect to come across on the internet are the 'opinions' of others and those who agree or disagree with them - more conflict, leaving us none the wiser.

We all have innate intelligence, but our authorities aren't leading with it - just look at what's happening to our world and how, by proxy, we're allowing them to do it. Our own intelligence grows when we choose to stop conforming to conventional standards; standards that history informs us are low indeed, and by recognising that we've created an ugly mess of the world - not by chance, not by accident, but willingly with full knowledge of the possible consequences. It's this mess that keeps us living in fear because we *know* where it eventually leads and we've been - and are still being - conditioned to feel powerless to do anything about it. Despite the horrible consequences of our apathy we wait, comply and support our tainted society, convinced that we're helpless or perhaps in need of some sort of salvation, that's always arriving … soon.

When we pick up a book to read, and aren't enjoying it - perhaps because we find it offensive, too violent or just plain boring, we put it down again or throw it into the bin; when we watch a film and dislike it for the same reasons we turn it off. However, when we see and think about all the 'bad' we've created in the world we do *nothing* against it, because we fear saying 'No' to our various authorities and losing what we've got - we can't see the bin or the off switch. We can say 'No' to a regime just as we do the book or film, or anything else for that matter - we *always* have a choice. It's only our 'what's the point' attitude and fear that pin us to our seats - fear of the imaginary consequences that have been instilled into us. Even if we're not spiritually minded it's clear that things aren't getting any better in the world and that our lives are going to come to an end at some point; it's a pretty good call to think about 'what happens next', rather than doing nothing or hedging our bets. Every one of us has the opportunity to change while we're still alive - to raise our vibration - and based on my personal experience I'd suggest that it's a good idea not to put that change off; we *must* keep moving by mental exercise - only then can we grow stronger, psychologically. Every moment is important because our heart beats for a limited time, and we don't know in advance when it's going to stop - the clock is ticking.

We spend our time here learning how things are from our parents and society; how we can best prepare ourselves to survive in this 'dog-eat-dog' world. Our education encourages us to compete with each other for the best paid jobs, in order to find security and purchase our own homes; it teaches us about the horrors of the past and how science will create a better future for us all. But science attempts to identify what can't be identified and to control what can't be controlled; it's limited and will *always* be limited because it relies on thought, which is limited; it's also under the control of an increasingly insane world that's going from strength to strength - nothing good can come from it until we grow 'up'. All the while, towns become more crowded, more and more people are without employment, corporations get richer and there's more and more disruption, confusion, corruption, perversion and separation going on in the world - online and off - *everybody* knows this. This is an over simplification of what's happening to our world right now, but as you're reading this book I prefer to credit you with enough intelligence to be aware of the rest, and to know that things aren't improving for ourselves or future generations. If we ignore a problem, it doesn't mean that it doesn't exist - it'll grow larger, fester and throb away in the back of our minds; it will ache in our hearts until *we* resolve it. Despite certain appearances and claims by our authorities, *no-one* is actually fighting for us, no-one ever has, no-one is indispensable in what they're doing; the battle we must *all* one day face is to overcome our apathy and *only* then can we come to know ourselves (as best we can) and until we do, the battle will continue to be played out and torment us. We must walk alone, but fight together - for One cause, instead of against each other.

~~~
~~~

Human beings have an innate need for companionship of some sort; if we're feeling lonely we turn on the television, message an internet 'friend' or play with apps on our mobile phones - as long as there's someone, or something, we can interact with; it doesn't necessarily have to be personal contact - what we need is to feel 'connected' in some way. Though we don't want to hear the negative and senseless chatter in our minds, there are times when we need to be alone and gather our thoughts for a while, which we don't mind doing as long as we know there's someone to talk to, should at any time we feel the need for it. In today's world being 'alone' for a while can be problematic, even when we're sleeping; it's difficult to be quiet when we're surrounded by noises and lights that are distracting - the hum of a refrigerator, the glow of an alarm clock, an incoming message, a neighbour returning home late or a car driving past can interfere with our peace - disturbance of some kind is very much a part of our world. We don't know *how* to be quiet, as noise has become so familiar to us that total silence can feel disorientating and frightening - a somewhat claustrophobic, alien and lonely experience, until we learn to enjoy being in our own company. We hear the noise of our minds more clearly when our surroundings are silent - we're then able to observe ourselves and see how uncomfortable we feel in our own company; this is the true meaning of loneliness. No-one feels lonely when at peace with themselves, but when we're not we can become desperate for a voice on the end of the phone, someone to socialise with, an outside activity, or a partner to keep us company - we always want a distraction of some kind.

On this journey we must be prepared, if necessary, to give up a lot - friends included. As we raise our consciousness level, the psychological distance between us and the people we know increases - we no longer speak the same language or have much in common; we're literally on a different wave length. At get-togethers for example, we may see a hand waving in this 'distance' and not know whether it's waving 'hello' or saying 'goodbye', but as our vibration rises we become more and more comfortable quietly observing our outside world (in all its madness) and with being alone - more and more comfortable with the silence that we find inside. The world no longer feels frightening or lonely and we no longer depend on outside activity for comfort or company - we see the hand waving and, in that moment, it matters not whether it's saying hello or goodbye.

The 'divine' and 'holy' are concepts that we dismiss with comments such as 'there's no old man with a beard sitting on a cloud looking down on us' - silly, because there isn't a person in the world who actually believes that there is. These comments and symbols are the tools we use to dismiss subjects we've made 'taboo' or 'weird'. They tend to be subjects that challenge the lifestyles we wish to pursue - the things we want to do without anyone tapping us on the shoulder. Though there's much to complain about in the world, we've no real wish to change - our fear of change is stronger than our curiosity or need to explore the contents of our minds. We're One; One world, One love, One consciousness, One family - One humanity trying hard to make sense of itself, and until we do we have One problem - love is missing from our lives. We must find this love again if we're ever going to live in peace, *first* for ourselves and only then for all others, but we can't find it if we continue to hold onto judgement, hatred, bitterness, jealousies, pain or other suffering - there's no place for these emotions when we live 'in Love'. None of us have any idea how long we'll remain in this particular 'existence', so we shouldn't miss the opportunity to let go of fear and its hand maidens, and surrender to Love, while we still can - our time is too short to be wasted.

'The greatest thing you'll ever
learn is just to love and be
loved in return.'

Nature Boy

Eben Ahbez

This isn't my home.
I'm just passing …
… through!
news ….. problems ….. work …
worry ….. fears ….. life

NOTES

NOTES

NOTES

NOTES

NOTES

About the Author

Renée Paule was born in London and was brought up in an orphanage, despite having two living parents. Subjected to mental and physical cruelty, the trauma she suffered left her with twelve years of almost total amnesia. Six marriages later (four official), she chose to 'take stock' and began a process of questioning everything in her world.

Her take on life changed dramatically following a profound experience revealing the connection between herself and the Universe - there's no separation. With this realisation, she no longer accepted the 'face-value' world she'd once thought of as the norm.

Renée Paule wishes to share this knowledge and show how a change of perspective can provide an alternative to the topsy-turvy world that Humanity, on the whole, accepts as an inevitable way of life.

She now lives in Ireland.

www.reneepaule.com

www.ingramcontent.com/pod-product-compliance
Lightning Source LLC
Chambersburg PA
CBHW021656070726
47591CB00017B/525